When a Child's Anxiety Takes Over
Second Edition

A Mother's Struggle to Save her
Child from Emetophobia

Micheline Cacciatore

When a Child's Anxiety Takes Over

Second Edition

 A Mother's Struggle to Save her Child from Emetophobia

Disclaimer: This book details the author's personal experiences with a child with anxiety and a specific phobia. The author is not licensed as a consultant, psychologist, or psychiatrist. This book is not intended as a substitute for consultation with a licensed mental health professional. Before you begin any change in your lifestyle in any way, you should consult a licensed professional to ensure that you are doing what's best for your situation.

Author's photo by Fabrizio Cacciator

Preface

I don't consider myself a writer. I have even said on many occasions over the years that I cannot write to save my life, but I have a story to share, so I am going to try.

I am a mother of two, a wife to my best friend, and a ballet teacher. Back in 2012, my life was turned upside down when my daughter developed severe anxiety and a phobia of vomit. Watching my daughter deteriorate both mentally and physically was the hardest thing I had ever experienced as a mother and the loneliness and fear that took over consumed my life. No one really understood our struggle and after tirelessly searching online for a parent who had been through this, I resigned to the fact that I would have to figure this out for myself.

A friend of mine said that it would help me to write things down, so I started a blog called *Emetophobia Deconstructed*. Writing down our daily struggles was helpful because it felt like my computer completely understood my struggle. It never gave me that confused look that I got from some people and it never gave me unwanted advice.

Each time I sat at my computer to type, I wished that someday another mother would find my blog and breathe a sigh of relief that they were no longer alone. I wanted to be that mother that I had searched for and let anyone with a child who was struggling with emetophobia know that they were not alone. A few weeks into my blog, my wish came true when I started getting comments from others who had our same struggle.

It is now three years after the start of my blog and I continue to receive emails and comments from families that have found themselves in a similar situation. Even though our struggle is thankfully in the past, their words of desperation and their gratitude for being able to read our story are a constant reminder of what we went through and how far we have come. I frequently hear from mothers who put into practice things that they have learned from our story and they happily share their progress.

All of this has prompted me to write this book so that I can reach out to more people. Our battle was so lonely and misunderstood, and my hope is that this book can help you or someone you know.

The Beginning

In 2011, my beautiful, magical, mysterious 10-year-old daughter became an emetophobic. I had never even heard of this phobia before. My spell check doesn't even recognize it on my computer as I look at the little red squiggly line under it. But believe me, it is very real.

Emetophobia is an intense and irrational fear pertaining to vomit. It is listed as one of the five most common phobias, yet it is rarely talked about. Not only are emetophobics afraid of vomit and the act of vomiting, but many other secondary phobias can arise. Anything that could possibly make an emetophobic gag, or choke, or get sick can become another fear. Secondary fears such as boats, germs, food, restaurants, going to the dentist, taking medicine, being in crowded places, and a fear of even leaving the safety of home can all become part of life for an emetophobic. All of these fears became part of our life. And life became miserable.

My daughter lost over 10 pounds within a few months, missed weeks of school, was afraid of food, afraid of her friends, and afraid of everyone in our family if we didn't wash our hands. All of this for a terrorizing fear that someone or something was going to make her sick and possibly vomit.

Why my daughter? I have some ideas. She was kind of hard wired with anxiety as soon as she was born. It's in our genes unfortunately. You know those babies you can never hand off to anyone else without piercing cries? The ones that never sleep and that cry much more than those other babies who are quietly resting in their own beds? That's my girl!

Born naturally in the water with a beloved midwife, she is our first child and the joy of our life (yes, even with all of the above) that we just wanted to hold and comfort and protect. We decided upon attachment parenting as the way to go. With lots of cuddles, she slept in our bed and was carried by my heart in my homemade sling.

We chose this method not only because I believed in it, but it was the only way to make her comfortable and happy. Sure, if I was willing to let my child cry it out for a year or two, maybe our lives would not have been such a struggle, but we couldn't do it. We tried. The doctor even said, "Babies cry. That's what they do. Just let her cry it out." I thought, *Really? All day and night? Are you sure?* After 9 months with that doctor, I didn't trust him anymore.

We changed doctors and found out that our poor little girl was suffering. She had allergies! She was lactose intolerant! What? Why the other doctor didn't test for these things still sickens me to this day. I look back and think of how I had to glue my child to me to make her feel comfortable when a simple diet change could have been all she needed to become a happy and independent child.

Undoing that glue has been quite a challenge over the years. Starting in kindergarten and lasting through 3rd grade, we had a serious separation anxiety problem. Getting her to school was a nightmare and I couldn't even go to the bathroom by myself until we found a child psychologist to help us. We solved that problem and life was much better with our wonderful little only child who enjoyed being the center of our world.

At the age of 7, her comfy little life got really uncomfortable. Our son was born. He was a surprise to us all, especially to her. Generalized anxiety started showing itself in lots of small ways, but it was nothing we couldn't handle with some extra comfort and some raising of our voices when necessary.

About 6 months after our son was born, my husband and I decided we needed a change. We wanted a warmer climate, a different job market for my husband, and I wanted to sell my ballet school. I didn't want any more nannies living in my house and I wanted to be able to spend more time with my children.

So, in June of 2010, we moved to Miami, FL. It was an exciting transition for my husband and me until five months after our move when I learned that nothing we had ever been through with our daughter could compare to a sudden bout of food poisoning.

Food Poisoning

One night in November of 2010 while my husband was away and I was tired of cooking, the kids and I went out to eat. It was not our usual type of destination for dinner, but this family restaurant chain was close by our new house. It was a far cry from our usual meal choices of spaghetti alle vongole, sushi or some other more refined restaurant options. We had fun stuffing ourselves with the kinds of food we don't usually go to restaurants for like mac and cheese and chicken fingers. We came home happy and full and went to bed.

In the middle of the night I was awakened by my daughter who was terrified because she had just thrown up her dinner on the floor. It was her first time throwing up since she was a baby when we tried to let her "cry it out" until she would throw up in her crib. Nice parents huh? We only tried that a few times. Doctor's orders!

I ran her into the bathroom because she didn't even understand that she was supposed to throw up in the toilet. It was a frantic scene because I really didn't want to clean vomit off the carpet in our new rental home. She was so distraught that she couldn't even think straight. She threw up a few more times and then we cuddled in my bed together and fell asleep.

I can't remember if it was the very next night that the panic attacks started or if things just got progressively worse over the next few months. It got to the point that she was absolutely terrified to go to sleep for fear of it happening again. We tried to help her rationalize and see how illogical she was being. That just because it happened once, doesn't mean it will happen again tonight. She is a very smart girl and knew the logic, but she just could not convince some part of her brain that was in panic mode. She would cry and shake at bedtime and was unable to get to bed before midnight most nights and was exhausted during the days.

She decided to become a vegetarian since she was now afraid of meat and she started checking the expiration dates on everything she ate. At first she seemed to be having severe anxiety only at night, but after a couple of months the anxiety started to become part of her daily life. She was scared of school if she knew someone was sick and she was also getting scared of going to ballet for the same reason. She was getting to the point where she just wanted to stay in the house where she felt safe.

Somewhere in these first couple of months my sister came to visit us and we set her up in our daughter's room so they could sleep together. This was when I realized the anxiety was even more troubling than I thought.

My daughter had a whole set of obsessive compulsive rituals that she was doing in her room every night. She was doing things like counting the fingers and toes on all her Barbie dolls and opening books to certain pages. She tried to hide them from my sister, but she noticed and promptly let me know. I was on the phone to find a psychologist the very next day.

Finding Help

A very kind and understanding psychologist named Dr. T got us right in to see her. She began cognitive behavioral therapy with my daughter, also known as CBT, as well as some training for my husband and me on how to deal with the situation at home. It was very hard to not lose our tempers. She would come out of her room in a panic at least five to ten times every night needing hugs and reassurance and we could not always keep from getting angry.

As therapy progressed, my daughter was slowly learning to use different techniques other than OCD rituals to fall asleep. She is a beautiful writer so I bought her a journal that she could write in before bed. However, that quickly turned into another ritual I later discovered when Dr. T suggested that I peek inside the journal. There were weeks' worth of pages where she wrote and drew exactly the same things on every page. Five hearts, ten stars, and so on. She believed that if she did these rituals, they would actually prevent her from throwing up.

When the OCD rituals started to get better, Dr. T wanted to slowly try an expose her to her fear of vomit. We began by simply saying words like vomit, puke, barf, throw up, etc. Initially she screamed and cried when we would say them but eventually she began to tolerate them. The idea was to expose her to her fear gradually and get her used to hearing the words without having such an intense reaction. This eventually led into some more difficult exposure therapy with Dr. T as they began to look at websites with photos of vomit. They started with cartoon images and slowly worked their way up to real life images.

Things were getting a bit more manageable after a few months of therapy. Her panic attacks were fewer but she was becoming more and more attached to me. She didn't miss any school days during this point, but she still preferred to stay home and be with us as much as possible after school and on weekends. She didn't want to help me anymore with my ballet classes for fear of all the little children and their germs and she avoided the ballet school as much as she could. This made me really sad since this had been our thing together for years. She grew up in our ballet school in Massachusetts. It was our home away from home.

Going on vacation also became extremely difficult. One of the reasons we moved to Miami was to be closer to our favorite island destination in Honduras and now she didn't want to go anymore. Our daughter who loved boats and snorkeling and fishing with Daddy was now terrified of the island. Why? Because some people get seasick! None of us have ever been seasick, but just knowing that some people do get sick on boats was enough for her. Our fun and livelihood on this tiny island where half the island is boat access only was no longer fun. We had been going there since she was 4 years old. My husband had business opportunities there and we were even planning to live there someday.

This was particularly hard for my husband to swallow. This island was his dream. It was his peace and solace from the regular hustle and bustle of life. It was my dream too, but on the back shelf for now since taking our daughter anywhere from her safety of home in Miami was getting to be one big tiring and mentally exhausting chore for me. After a couple of miserable trips to the island, I decided to stay home with the kids and let my husband go by himself when vacation and business opportunities arose. I was fine with that because it was so much easier for me.

After about a year of therapy we were still seeing Dr. T on a weekly basis. Summer break from school was approaching, and with some encouragement from Dr. T, we reluctantly booked a trip to our favorite little island. I was hesitant, but prepared, for 3 weeks of her anxieties away from the comforts of home. Dr. T worked with her a lot and helped to prepare her for the trip.

On our previous trip to Honduras we had promised our daughter we would never take the ferry from the mainland to the island if the seas were not calm. It can be an awful trip in rough seas. When we arrived to the mainland of Honduras for that last trip my husband checked the buoy report just like he promised. The forecast was for calm flat seas. Unfortunately, we learned that the buoy reports in Honduras were NOT a reliable source of information and as soon as we got out to sea it was a horrible one hour trip with 12 foot waves. She spent the hour outside with my husband at the back of the boat screaming and crying, while I was on the inside with my son who was having a blast rocking with the waves. The boat workers were handing out vomit bags and plenty of passengers were using them. That was the last time we went to the island and it was a miserable three weeks.

This time we made sure to book our favorite pilot for a private plane ride from the mainland. We were determined to make this a good trip for all of us. If we counted all the money we have spent during these past few years on psychologists, a psychiatrist, an anxiety clinic, and private airplanes instead of boats, we could have our own private island by now!

Once we settled into our house on the island I was a bit surprised to see that she was happy to be there. She seemed fairly calm and ready for the adventure. She was not ready to hop on our little boat yet but I could see her constantly looking at the ocean from our deck. I watched her trying to calculate in her head how much the boat would rock if the seas were wavy. My husband went fishing on the boat and we watched him with our binoculars.

Over the next few days we had fun visiting our friends that live on the island. My daughter offered to babysit her little brother along with our friend's children whom she adored. While she babysat, my husband and I were able to go out on the boat together and have some fun.

The next day we found out that one of the kids she babysat threw up that night. Then his brother and one of the other kids began throwing up that day. No! This was the last thing I needed her to find out. Our friends all knew about her phobia and we were all messaging each other to keep it a secret. Part of me was thinking that she needed to get this stomach virus that was going around. Throwing up again could be the cure. Our psychologist had mentioned that in the past, but I could not think like that yet. Not when I had no Dr. T in case things went really wrong. We stayed away from our friends for a few days and remained thankful that none of us got sick.

After a few days she was still doing really well and we were actually able to get her on our boat. We started by staying in the harbor the first time and then taking longer trips each day. She was doing it! She was quiet and pensive, but she was calm. I took a photo of her sitting on the bow of the boat and I felt some peace. I was happy that she was happy. I was happy that I was on the boat and able to relax and enjoy myself and my family instead of having to distract and console and comfort her. As soon as we got back to the house I sent the photo in an email to Dr. T. I thanked her for her work and let her know how happy I was that I was slowly getting my child back!

We had a great few weeks on the island and then returned home to enjoy the rest of summer while getting ready for the start of middle school. Little did I know that middle school and all the added pressures of homework, a new school and new friends would bring it all on again. I was warned by Dr. T that it could be hard at first, but I had no idea how bad it was going to get.

Middle School Begins

Middle school began in August of 2012. She was at a new school that was very different from her tiny Waldorf style school where there was no homework, tests, grades or academic pressure. She was now in a very academic private school with a lot more students than she was used to.

She was excited to be in this new beautiful school and was settling in quite nicely during the first week of school. She loved the students and the teachers much better than her last school and she liked getting more of an academic challenge. However, towards the end of the second week of school, someone threw up in the hallway and that was all it took to bring it all back.

Her anxiety took a turn for the worst. She started thinking about the amount of kids in school and the amount of germs there must be. Not to mention that in middle school, someone is always complaining of a headache or a stomach ache or some kind of ailment. She started washing her hands a lot. A lot! And she started thinking she was sick every day or was going to get sick from whoever was near her at school. Her brain, whether consciously or not, came up with a plan to be able to control her from getting sick. Mind you I am not a psychologist, but I was picking my own brain for answers and explanations.

Suddenly school became a dangerous place. She needed to not eat there, stay out of the bathrooms, carry hand sanitizer, and steer clear of the janitors who must be full of germs. She would even hold her breath when walking through crowds of students.

She distanced herself from her friends, especially if they complained of any ailments, and would call me from school if she found out someone was sick. I had to pick her up one day when she overheard a boy talking about how his little brother threw up the night before. She was in the hallway crying and her teacher could not convince her to come back into the classroom.

She would have stomach aches every morning because she was so terrified and would beg and plead us not to take her to school. She would constantly make us promise her she was not going to get sick and would not relax until we did. We were getting her to schools most days, but she was consistently late and would refuse to eat breakfast.

In addition to all of this, she tried to stay away from her little brother who must be bringing home lots of germs from preschool. She would ask us when we washed his hands and our hands and when I cleaned the kitchen counters and what did I use to clean them. She started to check expiration dates on everything. She was doing that for a while, but now the expiration date had to be far away in order for her to eat something. She ate very little, had to inspect everything she ate, and going out for dinner was becoming quite a chore.

One night we went to one of our favorite Italian restaurants. We know the owner, it's very clean, and the food is great. We sat outside and she promptly got up to go wash her hands. She came back quickly and in a panic because the bathroom was locked and she couldn't get in. She was crying and shaking and begging us to go home. She said there were too many people and too many germs. She needed to get out! I look around and it was still early for dinner in Miami Beach. There was maybe one other couple at a nearby table and we were outside in the fresh air. I pointed this all out to her and I got her to calm down. I told her we were not going home and I walked her to the bathroom so she could wash her hands. When we got back to the table she started asking me how we would know if the chef or the waiters were sick. Ugh. That was the last time we went out for dinner for a while.

School was becoming an almost impossible task and she stopped going to her ballet classes. She was getting to school maybe two or three days out of each week and would tell me she did not feel well every single morning. She would stay in the bathroom for a while and convince me some days that she needed to stay home because she felt sick. I explained to her that it was the anxiety starting to hurt her tummy for real.

She made me promise her every morning and every night that she wouldn't get sick. I knew it was an empty promise and it killed me to do so, but if I didn't do it, there was severe panic. Her hands were now cracked and bleeding from all of the washing and she was taking two showers a day instead of her one ritual before bedtime shower. What the heck was happening? Things were completely out of control.

We were now seeing Dr. T every week instead of every other week which we started after our summer vacation when she was doing so well. Dr. T explained to me that my daughter now needed medication because she was no longer able to put anything in practice that Dr. T was doing with her. She was angry and sad all the time and her weight was down to 58 lbs. That is not even at the 0 percentile on the growth chart! She was 65.5 lbs.

at the start of school just two months ago. She looked awful with gray circles under her eyes and not an ounce of fat on her.

I sat on Dr. T's couch and cried like a baby. Medication? No way. My husband had been pushing for it since she was born practically, and I wanted no part of it. There can be horrible side effects. I knew kids who had been on them and two of them ended up in hospitals because of suicidal thoughts. No! I am the "O' Natural" lady. I birthed my kids at home, chose attachment parenting, and I have cabinets full of homeopathic medicine. I needed a better plan.

To appease my husband and Dr. T's professional opinion, I started calling psychiatrists. A very frustrating task I quickly found out. I called the one she gave me the name of first. After waiting two days, and no call back, I tried again sounding more desperate. Finally she called me back and told me she had no openings. She gave me five other names and I called them all. My husband was now getting mad at me for not being able to produce an appointment. Not mad, maybe just frustrated with my stubbornness and not listening to him years ago.

A few more days went by and one psychiatrist finally called me back and said she had an opening. She also said she does not take any insurance, her fee was $300 per session, and she needed about four or five sessions to come up with a diagnosis and a plan. She was also not willing to work together with Dr. T. Okay, now I felt like *I* was going to throw up!

I did some more research on the computer and I came across a website I had seen in the past. "Is your child feeling anxious or sad? Is it affecting their daily life?" Hell yes! I picked up my phone and I called The Child and Adolescent Mood and Anxiety Treatment Program at the University of Miami, also known as CAMAT. I had a 30-minute phone interview with a very nice man. I told him I was desperate. He told me his boss was out of town until Monday and I would have to wait until early next week to find out if my daughter would be a good candidate to be evaluated for their program. The waiting game started again.

Much to my surprise he called me back 30 minutes later telling me that he called his boss and she gave him the okay to get my daughter in. I must have sounded desperate! The earliest evaluation appointment they had was two weeks away. I resigned to the fact that this was going to be a long process and I accepted that we had to hang in there. I relayed my new plan to my husband and Dr. T and they both said, "That's great! But do you have an appointment with a psychiatrist in the meantime?" I told Dr. T my dilemma with trying to find one and that I was done with that for now. I said I was going to wait to hear what the clinic at the University of Miami had to say first.

In the meantime, things were getting worse and my husband started looking online for psychiatrists. He found one that actually called him back and left a message. They played phone tag for a few days until my husband had to leave the country for a quick trip. I took over and got an appointment with this 75 year old man who worked two days per week and was an hour away. I made the appointment but thought there must be a better option.

Last Hope for Help

The day finally arrived for our four hour evaluation at the Child and Adolescent Mood and Anxiety Treatment program (CAMAT). I felt a small sense of relief that things were starting to be put into place. The clinicians spent two hours with our daughter and another two hours with my husband and me.

One clinician was a graduate student at the University and the other had her PhD and was doing a fellowship at the clinic. They needed to get an entire history and try to narrow down the problem so they could come up with a more specific diagnosis and a treatment plan.

For a while it was a mishmash of generalized anxiety disorder, separation anxiety, a specific phobia, and OCD with all of the hand washing and other rituals. When the appointment ended we left there exhausted from all of their questions. I was given an appointment for the following week to hear their feedback and hopefully a treatment plan.

In the meantime, we were still struggling with school and her daily ailments. One day she had convinced herself she had salmonella poisoning because we had chicken for dinner the night before. Ugh, another missed day of school. I was getting automated emails every day from the school about missed classes and grades and my daughter was getting thinner, depressed, and angry.

Knowing we had to wait another week or so for the CAMAT appointment, I hopped onto the computer again and typed in *child psychiatrists Miami.* There were all of the names I had already called and then one popped right out at me that I didn't see before and I gave her a call. She called me back right away and told me she had a cancellation and could see us the very next day. I canceled the appointment with the old man my husband had found and breathed a huge sigh of relief. Help was just around the corner, I hoped.

This psychiatrist was wonderful. She saw that I was terrified of medication and she explained that she is a very conservative neuropsychiatrist. After talking with my daughter and me, she absolutely saw the need for some medication and explained that it would take about three to six weeks to show any effects. She handed me the prescription and my eyes welled up with tears. It was half of the usual pediatric dosage of sertraline so I was a bit at ease. She explained that my daughter would start at a low dose and then slowly work her way up to a full pediatric dose. Her body needed to slowly get used to it and she didn't want to induce any side effects such as nausea.

We picked up the medicine from the pharmacy and went directly to Dr. T so she could work with her on actually taking the medicine. That was another huge problem. My daughter would not take medicine of any kind because she was afraid she would gag and throw up. A few weeks before this we had a crazy visit to the ER for an asthma episode. It turned into a nightmare when they had to give her injections because she refused to take the medicine. One doctor and three nurses had her in a panic trying to get her to take medicine. They realized I spoke the truth when they finally gave up for fear of her having a serious panic attack and possibly harming them and/or herself.

We arrived at Dr. T's office and she got her to crush up a tiny pill and put it in some applesauce. It took them the entire hour appointment, but Dr. T was able to accomplish the nearly impossible. I breathed a sigh of relief knowing that we would not have a battle at home over taking the medicine.

The feedback appointment at the clinic was a couple days later. I met with Dr. G, the PhD psychologist who did our evaluation. She explained to me that the diagnosis they all agreed upon was a specific phobia of vomit. They would keep their eyes open for obsessive compulsive disorder and separation anxiety, but they believed that those were just symptoms of the phobia. It all sounded quite logical to me and I was so impressed with this young doctor. She had a way of explaining things to me that seemed so clear and easy to understand.

She explained the treatment plan of intensive daily exposure therapy for about four hours each day. My daughter would need to be taken out of school for at least two weeks and then be gradually introduced back. She would be exposed to public bathrooms and germs and would eventually be exposed to vomit.

I felt like I was throwing my child to the lions and that she was going to get eaten alive. I was afraid that a graduate student would be the one working with my daughter instead of a psychologist and I was very hesitant. Dr. G explained that she would be the one doing all of the therapy under the direction of the CAMAT director. I knew this was our last hope and I really had no other choice but to put my trust in her.

My head was spinning as I wondered how on earth my daughter would catch up with all the missed school. I was also thinking about our trip to Massachusetts the following week to spend Thanksgiving with my family. How was this all going to work?

Then, because my head was not spinning enough, Dr. G told me the price. I didn't even have any words and I started to cry. Our life was so upside down right now. We moved to Miami to save money! My husband was struggling to make his new real estate career become profitable and we were spending money on private school for our daughter that was not in our budget because our local public school was not a safe place. I had a weekly psychologist fee and now a psychiatrist fee as well as medication to pay for. I also had a 14 yr. old chocolate lab at home waiting for me to take him to the vet to fix an eye infection we had been ignoring. And, now this. It was more than I was expecting, although she explained that it was less than a private psychological or hospital clinic since the CAMAT program is part of a research program within the University's Psychology Department.

Dr. G gave me a few moments to call my husband who was away and talk it over with him. Of course we both realized that our life could not go on as is and we had to accept this therapy option. I signed the papers and felt a knot in my stomach. It was so hard not to look at our daughter as this child that was making our daily lives miserable and our finances dwindle. It's such a terrible feeling to have a hard time loving the very thing you should love the most.

We ended the meeting with the fact that we both had to look at our schedules and come up with a start date. Dr. G had to clear two weeks of her schedule to work with us and I needed to think long and hard about this because I was supposed to be on a plane with the kids in a week and a half to visit my family for Thanksgiving. A trip that my daughter was already terrified of because of airplane germs and the fact that she would be seeing her cousin who was frequently sick. If we went on this trip it would mean that we could not start therapy until after the Thanksgiving and Christmas holidays since once we started, there could be no breaks. I honestly didn't think we would make it another week without some serious help. She was losing weight daily and it was getting medically dangerous.

When I got home I got on the phone and started begging the airline to allow me to change my ticket and not have to pay any fees. I could not afford anymore fees! They were really kind as I told them our crazy story. They waived all fees and gave me travel vouchers for the full amount I paid.

I then went to my daughter's school to talk with her guidance counselor. I explained that she was going to be missing two to three weeks of school and was going to have to start back slowly with half days after that. It was her first year at this school and they had only known her for a few months. I was fearful that they were going to tell me they were not equipped to handle this kind of situation and would ask me to withdraw her from the school. My daughter had left early in tears most days so far and had horrible attendance. I was so relieved when the counselor told me not to worry and that they would work with us. She said they knew from her entrance exam and her schoolwork so far that she was a bright girl just going through a rough time. We made a plan that would allow her to work from home and email her assignments to her teachers. All quizzes and tests could be made up when she returned to school.

On the way home I called Dr. T to let her know how my meeting at CAMAT went. I told her what the recommendation was and I asked her what her opinion was since I was scared about how intense this therapy sounded. She was also concerned because she thought it could be too intense and possibly make things worse. This did not ease my fears but I knew nothing else was working and I was not willing to look at medication as a long term thing.

When I got home I called my family back in Massachusetts. My sister had a feeling we would have to cancel our trip and she was very supportive. My Mom was amazing, too. She was scared for her granddaughter's health and cried with me on the phone. I can imagine it must have been hard to hear all this from far away and not be able to fully understand the daily struggles we had and how we were dealing with them. I think no one in my family really understood how serious this all was until then.

My final call that day was to Dr. G. I told her that I had cleared our schedule and we were ready to start on Monday.

Intensive Daily Therapy Begins

I dropped my son off at pre-school on Monday, November 12th, and made plans for my friend to pick him up after school. I met my husband and daughter at the clinic and he and I had a meeting with Dr. G first. She told us what she would be doing with our daughter for the next few hours and explained that we would all meet again for the last 45 minutes so that our daughter could teach us everything she learned. This would be helpful for us, and for her, and for Dr. G so she knew that our daughter was grasping things.

We arrived back for our meeting and learned a lot from our daughter about the specific physiological responses of the body when it is anxious and in fight or flight mode. This helped her to understand why she would get headaches, dizziness, shortness of breath, excessive yawning, sweaty and numb hands, stomach aches, vibrating arms, a racing heart, and all the other things that would happen when she was anxious or having a panic attack.

She was taught how to scan her body and really sit with and feel her physiological responses instead of being scared of them or trying to distract herself from them. They also worked on understanding an anxiety scale and how to rate her anxiety in specific situations. On paper, it looked like a thermometer. Zero was no anxiety, and eight was the highest level of anxiety.

We were so impressed with how much she had learned and the way in which she was able to teach us. She had learned some of this in the past with Dr. T, but not in such an intense and school like manner. There were papers all over the table that they had been working on.

I learned a lot from her as well. One important thing I learned this day was that all of those relaxation techniques she had been taught in the past were not to be used anymore. They never worked anyway and always seemed to turn into rituals. She was now supposed to pay attention to her anxiety and learn to recognize it and feel when it was going down.

Towards the end of our meeting, Dr. G started to talk to her about the next steps they would be taking. Not specifics, but just generally about how people have to face their fears when they are scared of something. She told her that the next day they were going to be detectives. I could see her starting to get a bit nervous. I started sweating, too. I knew the next steps and I was afraid I would have to physically place my child in the car to get her here when things would start getting more intense.

We had a nice talk in the car on the way home and we told her how proud of her we were. We talked about how Dr. G is so young and cute and likable and how she wants to be psychologist just like her someday. Little did my daughter know, she was not going to have such kind words about Dr. G in a few days.

The next day we headed back to the clinic again. It was the same routine as yesterday and we left her there and came back towards the end. When we returned, we learned that they had started to do some detective work. After we met all together, my husband and I met with Dr. G alone. This is the meeting we learned that we were no longer allowed to answer our daughter's usual questions about getting sick and about germs. Dr. G told us that we were no longer allowed to reassure her that she was not going to get sick because she had learned a new skill that she needed to practice called "detective thinking."

Basically, when a thought entered her mind she had to write it down and then write down any evidence both for and against the thought. For example, the thought may be: *I will not go into a public bathroom because I will get sick.* Evidence to support the thought: Someone could get sick from germs in a public bathroom. Evidence against the thought: Most people do not get sick from public bathrooms and I have never gotten sick from a public bathroom. They practiced this with many different thoughts and we learned that she is the one who needs to think through each thought and use her own brain instead of ours. Taking control over her own thoughts and actions was a very important step.

When we met all together again, Dr. G explained to our daughter how no one can guarantee that she will not throw up again, and in fact, it is almost a guarantee that she WILL throw up again someday. She helped our daughter understand that we would be lying to her if we made that guarantee.

When we left the clinic she was very mad. She started to ask us her usual questions and we replied with "It's time to use your detective thinking." She told us how she didn't like this anymore and how she didn't want to go back. She started getting really angry with us when we wouldn't ease her fears about her usual daily anxiety provoked questions. Am I going to get sick from dinner? Where did you buy the food? Is the food expired? When did you wash your hands? Was anyone sick at her little brother's school? There were all of her usual questions, but there was no more of us answering them.

One day during this first week of therapy my daughter told me that she wanted to keep her phobia. She loved it and she was not going to let this Dr. G lady take it away. As I thought about that insane statement, I asked her if she loved the phobia because it was keeping her safe from getting sick. It made sense in her mind I guess. Her phobia made her wash her hands, it kept her from dangerous places like school, and it had her on the lookout 24/7. It was her control and she was not going to let it go without a fight. And it seemed like fighting was the only thing going on between us. We were battling over the soap, the showers, the food, and everything.

The next days were harder to get her to the clinic. She was mad and resistant, but she got there without too much drama. Dr. G began taking her to the bathrooms in the building to perform different tasks. They started with simply walking into different bathrooms and then building up to touching things in the bathrooms and delaying hand washing. She had to write down the tasks and practice rating her anxiety. She was forced to use her detective thinking and write down her thoughts and physiological feelings during every task. We met all together at the end of each day and Dr. G explained the homework of working on some tasks at home and writing about them.

On the second or third day during one of our end of the day meetings, Dr. G was in the middle of explaining the homework tasks when she took a sip of her water and started coughing. She was coughing as if the water went down the wrong side of her throat, but she was totally faking it. She was holding, and coughing on, one of those fun pens that click to change colors and I didn't realize her plan until after the fact. When she was done with her coughing episode, she said to my daughter, who didn't really catch that she had coughed all over the pen, "And here is a fun pen to do your homework with!" Then, ever so perfectly, Dr. G slid the pen across the table to my daughter so that she had to catch it to avoid it falling on the floor. When she caught it and put it into her bag, Dr. G made sure she knew she coughed all over the pen. I could see the instant fear in my daughter's eyes. She asked Dr. G if she was sick, and her reply of course, was "I guess you'll have to use your detective thinking…"

Thankfully we only lived five minutes from the clinic at the time since it was not a fun ride home. In the car, she started talking about another serious fear that she had which was of harming herself. In the beginning of the school year, there was a seminar about bullying in which they talked about, and showed illustrated photos of kids that had killed themselves. She was haunted by those images so much that I had to call the school and ask them to find somewhere else for her to be during those seminars.

When she was having moments of anxiety she would say things like, "I am afraid I will do something like that even though I know I won't." She had been saying things like that for the past couple of months and Dr. T said that it was just the anxiety talking, but to keep an eye out. She told me to take her to the hospital if we were ever concerned that she would hurt herself. We were never concerned that she would actually act on these thoughts. However, I was getting concerned now because she started digging her nails into her skin and biting herself when she was feeling out of control. She said she couldn't stop thinking about the kids that had killed themselves.

Things seemed to be getting more and more out of control. She started washing her hands more frequently and they were cracked, bleeding, and full of rashes. Dr. G said that things would get worse before they got better, but this was really hard to watch and know how to deal with.

That night we were supposed to do some written homework that Dr. G had assigned. When she refused, I took "the pen" that Dr. G coughed all over and my daughter's homework papers from her bag and we did it together with me writing everything. I had promised her a back massage after we did the homework, but once she realized I used "the pen" she wouldn't let me touch her. She was so mad at me because I would not wash my hands and mad because she really wanted that back massage and could not control the situation.

Towards the end of our first week at the clinic we had a short break since Dr. G was going away for a conference. I had a blood test set up for my daughter that was ordered by the psychiatrist and Dr. G thought this was a great homework task. Going to a doctor's office where there are sick people and germs! Dr. G told us to make sure we do some homework papers about the task and also told me to not let her wash her hands or shower immediately after the doctor visit. The plan was that she would have to wait 30 minutes once we got home.

Physical and Blood Test

I made the doctor's appointment for first thing in the morning because I knew there would be less people. As soon as we walked into the waiting room my daughter started following me like a puppy. I couldn't even check her in or get my insurance card out easily because she was so close to me. I asked her to sit down a number of times before she finally found a seat by the door. She had her sweater over her face so she wouldn't breathe in any germs. I reminded her that this was a homework task and that she needed to remove her sweater and breathe properly. She had been known to hold her breath when she walked past people that she thought could be sick or even if she walked through a crowd of people.

I saw the doctor first so I could give her a quick history. This was the first time I brought my daughter to my doctor. There was no way I was going to get her to her pediatrician's office. That office was always full of sick children and the waiting room was pretty small.

The doctor then met with both of us. She checked her weight and height and did a quick physical. She noticed her hands that were red and cracked and then she took us to the blood lab. There was a nurse waiting for us and my daughter started getting really nervous. We sat my daughter on my lap and the doctor pulled up a chair in front of us because she realized she was going to have to help. Usually she would have gone out to see other patients at this point, but she was amazing and perceptive. She is also an ER doctor and is used to kids who are fearful.

While she sat on my lap she started begging everyone to wait. She said she just needed time to breathe. We gave her a minute but when she begged for longer we had to say no. I had my arms wrapped around her tightly and the doctor held out her arm for the nurse to put the needle into. She screamed and struggled but was so meek at 11 years old and 56 lbs. that we were able to restrain her pretty easily.

She was so distraught that the doctor wanted to do an ECG. They repeated it two or three times because the readings were so crazy. The nurse stayed with her while the doctor took me into another room. She told me that this phobia needed to be solved ASAP. I broke down in tears when she handed me a copy of the ECG to take home. It said: abnormal ECG; enlarged left ventricle. I asked the doctor what that meant and she said it was from stress. We agreed it should be repeated again soon to see if there would be any change.

When we got into the car to go home she talked about her need to wash her hands and shower immediately. I reminded her that she had to eat breakfast and take her medicine first and then she could shower. Waiting to wash hands and waiting to shower was a task we had been working on for a couple of days. She got really mad and said she was afraid because she was thinking about the images of the kids that killed themselves from school again.

We got home and she sat at the dining room table. I will never forget the look in her eyes at that moment. She turned from my scared helpless little girl to an angry and hurtful person. She told me that she was not going to eat until I let her take a shower and that I would have to watch her starve to death. Remembering what I had been coached to say by Dr. G, I said "I know it must be hard." Then I ignored her as instructed to do many times by Dr. T and now Dr. G.

She started yelling that she hated me and that I was a horrible mother. I tried to keep busy by putting dishes away and cleaning the kitchen. I purposely did not wash my hands first, and when she noticed, she started yelling at me to wash them and saying she would never eat off of those dishes again. I was trying to ignore her, but it was so hard. My back was to her and tears were streaming down my cheeks as she told me how she hated me and how she would starve herself to death. I couldn't take it anymore and I lost control. I was shaking and crying and yelling at her that I couldn't do this anymore. I threatened her by telling her how she would not be able to live in our home if she could not follow the rules. I shocked the hell out of her and myself.

To my surprise, she went to the fridge and took out the pasta that she refused to eat the night before because there was sausage in it. She warmed it up herself and ate it. Then she asked me for her medicine. I gave it to her and then I went to my room to put away days of piled up laundry.

After she took her medicine, she very nicely came and asked if she could help me. We exchanged a much needed apology and did some homework about the task of going to the doctor. When she went to go take a shower, I laid in my bed crying because I seriously thought I couldn't do this. I may not be as strong as I thought I was.

Dr. G called that afternoon from her conference to check on us. I told her what happened, including my temper tantrum, and we agreed that she would call us the next day and check in again. We made it through the night without any more battles, but she refused to do any more homework and I didn't push.

First Week of Therapy Finished

The next day was pretty horrible. My daughter was mad and argumentative about everything and I could not get her to do any of the homework tasks. She was supposed to be washing her hands less, going out into public to open doors, going into public bathrooms, and spinning in a chair until she gets dizzy. In addition to not even wanting to leave the house, she was having episodes of being afraid to be alone because she would think about killing herself.

Dr. G called us in the morning from the airport to check on things. She said she would call us again when she returned to Miami that afternoon so we could talk more. I was happy that she called us frequently. She was my sanity.

My husband was getting ready to leave for the island in Honduras the next day for some real estate business and I was a mess. He had offered numerous times to cancel his trip, but I wouldn't let him. He was going with a good friend of ours, and they would both lose their money. I was pretty sure I could handle things. I always did in the past, although I was a bit worried this time. I was also hoping that the medicine my daughter started taking two weeks ago would kick in soon.

Dr. G called us when her plane landed and she decided that we should come into the clinic for a bit so we could have a clear plan for the weekend. My daughter and I showed up at the clinic at 5:00 on a Friday afternoon and Dr. G whipped out a notebook full of ideas that she had written down during her flight. At that moment, I felt that our money was really being put to good use. I didn't think anyone would put this much effort into helping us. She had a clear plan about completing some specific tasks along with some new things to try, but more importantly, we talked about my daughter's thoughts and words about suicide.

They had had a conversation about suicide together before Dr. G went away and my daughter realized that she was saying these things not because she was planning on doing anything, but mainly because she felt completely out of control. Dr. G taught her other ways to say that she needed a break if she was feeling out of control. My husband and I were also told earlier that week that if she talked about killing herself, we were supposed to take her to the emergency room.

We knew she was not going to do anything, and we didn't take her to the hospital when she would slip and say something. Dr. G came up with a contract that we all had to sign that afternoon. It basically said that my husband and I must take her to the emergency room the moment she says anything related to harming herself again. She explained to my daughter that talking about hurting herself was a very serious thing. If she meant it, then she needed to say it, but if she didn't mean it, then she needed to find other words.

Dr. G told her the story of *The Boy Who Cried Wolf* and was very clear to the two of us how serious this was. She made us both sign the contract and we brought it home for my husband to sign as well. I tacked it up on our kitchen bulletin board in clear view.

Knowing the horrible week we had, and the fact that my husband was leaving in the morning, our friends offered to come over and watch the kids so we could have a quiet dinner out together. I would love to say our dinner was romantic and relaxing, but we were both stressed out beyond belief. He was worried about leaving me for the week and I was simply distraught about our daughter.

As stressed as we were, it was really nice to be together away from the house. We had just celebrated 16 years of marriage and I love him than I have words for. It felt like our daughter was tearing us apart at times and it was often hard to be on the same page about how to deal with her and how to deal with our emotions. He was busy working, traveling, and taking care of our son and I was the one dealing with our daughter and meeting with Dr. G.

After my husband left for his trip, the first task of the weekend was for her to come to the ballet studio with my son and me. I teach a lot of young children on Saturdays and this was a hard task for her. She managed pretty well by keeping the door to outside open for some fresh air. We spent the rest of the afternoon at home catching up on some school work and our other task of looking at photos of vomit online.

Our task for Sunday was to go to the mall. The outdoor mall, since the indoor one was out of the question for now. In addition to buying prizes for a new reward system, our tasks were to get there, go into a bathroom and just use the sink to rinse her hands. She was also supposed to open all of the doors of the stores we would visit so she could get used to touching handles again.

As soon as we entered the parking lot, she got a stomach ache and wanted to go home. I told her we could go home as soon as we got the tasks done. We headed to the bathroom first and I had to gently push her in when she refused. She put one hand under the faucet quickly and then I had to coach her to use both hands. She did it but then frantically ran out of the bathroom using her shirt to open the door before my son and I were even finished. We got all the other tasks done and headed home.

When we got home, I had her wait 15 minutes before she was allowed to shower. She washed her hands a lot while she waited. They were so red and it made me sad to even look at them. We spent the rest of the day at home and we set up a box with her new prizes of nail polish, earrings, and all sorts of other fun things we found. I let her shower while I put my son to bed and then we had plans to watch a movie together. This was her second shower of the day. The shower before bed was her one ritual that she had kept for the past 2 years and I was not going to mess with it. I had tried before.

When she got out of the shower I braided her hair and we set up the *Harry Potter* movie that she wanted to watch. Suddenly, she needed to wash her hands again as we sat down to watch the movie. I told her she could rinse them with water, but no soap. She started to panic and I put the soap away. Now I had a battle on my hands as she continued to yell that she needed to wash her hands.

She went to the bathroom and I heard the water turn on and the cabinet open. When she came out she told me she didn't use any soap. I went into the bathroom and saw a wet cabinet handle that I opened to find a wet container of soap that was dry when I had put it under the sink. I asked her if she used it and again she said no. I pointed out the obvious and she still denied.

She sat on the couch and looked at me with evil eyes and arms crossed. She yelled that she hated me and she hated Dr. G and she was never going back to the clinic. I asked her to quiet down because her brother was sleeping but she got louder and louder and was saying horrible things to me. I tried to ignore as I was supposed to do but she wouldn't stop. My blood pressure was rising and my hands were shaking. I asked her again to be quiet and she got louder and meaner. Then I told her to go to her room and she wouldn't. I didn't know what to do! I stood up and walked towards her. She got up to yell at me more and I slapped her on the bum and told her to stop. She still wouldn't stop so I turned off the lights and the TV and I said goodnight.

I went to my room and locked my door. I realized I had lost my temper again but I didn't know what else to do. This ignoring business did not work. I tried it so many times until I eventually wound up losing control. She came to my door a few minutes later and apologized for lying and for saying all those mean things. We hugged and went back to the couch to watch a bit of the movie before bed.

Exposure Therapy Week Two

Monday, November 19th, was the start of our second week at the clinic. It was Thanksgiving week, so we only had three days of therapy that week. This was the week that the more intense exposures would begin.

After my explosion last night, I wanted to talk to Dr. G alone first and just get some reminders of what I needed to do to keep my cool and not lose my temper. Our previous psychologist always gave me great advice that would keep me calm from week to week. Dr. T knew me really well and knew what kind of parent I was and that I am not abusive in any way, shape, or form.

Unfortunately, I realized Dr. G did not know me that well yet. She listened and immediately asked if I left any marks on my daughter when I slapped her. My heart skipped a beat and I suddenly realized her concern. Of course I did not leave any marks. It was an open handed spank through her clothes.

We got past that and she reminded me of what I needed to be doing. I was reminded that my daughter wanted to get a rise out of me. It was a form of attention for her. She told me that I was like vending a machine and my daughter was going to shake me until she got what she wanted. I just needed to ignore, ignore, ignore. I thanked her for the advice and I left them to do their therapy for the next few hours.

They began by visiting bathrooms again and going into the stalls to touch things. Dr. G had her touch the sanitary napkin disposal in the stall because my daughter didn't know what it was and was afraid. She thought it was for throw up bags. My daughter spent most of that day crying in the bathroom with Dr. G never answering her as to what this little garbage was for. She was supposed to be using her detective thinking and be able to rate her anxiety and cope with what she was feeling and being asked to accomplish.

When I met with Dr. G by myself at the end of the day, she told me not to answer any of my daughter's questions about the sanitary napkin disposal but to let her figure it out on her own. I noticed that Dr. G was not really looking at me while she was talking. She was kind of gazing out the window a bit which seemed unusual for her, but I figured she was tired from a long morning with my crazy child.

I thought our meeting was almost done and then the conversation shifted. She was now looking at me straight in the eyes. She told me how she had a talk with the director and they were concerned about my daughter's safety at home. My heart stopped and my stomach churned. She explained about how they are supposed to report any abuse if they think it is necessary. I didn't even know what to say. I felt sick and really uncomfortable. This was the most unhelpful thing anyone had ever said to me and I sat there sweating and trying to convince her that I was not going to harm my kids. She was questioning my parenting skills and she asked me if I am a parent that leads my children around by their arms. My head was spinning and I didn't even know what she meant by that. No! I am a damn good parent that lives and breathes for my kids! Am I not allowed to lose my temper? Ever?

She had a pen and paper in hand and was asking me who I knew that could come over to our house that night to make sure I wouldn't do anything horrible. She knew my husband was away and there was no one else. My best friend was teaching until late, and another friend, who had taken my son in as her third child during all of this, was away for Thanksgiving.

She was pressuring me for a name while looking down at her paper waiting for me to produce one. I had to tip my head down to look her in the eyes and I said, "Look, I just moved here not too long ago. I am busy with two kids and I have no other friends close by. Do you know how hard it is to start over again in a new state and find friends in the middle of all of this? There is no one! I am not going to hurt my kids!" I told her that my mother is a therapist and I would call her for some advice if I was feeling stressed. That was good enough for her and it was never talked about again.

I said nothing about my conversation with Dr. G to my daughter. We had a horrible car ride home because she was so mad at me for making her do all of this and she told me again how much she hated Dr. G and how she was not going back there. When we got home she immediately showered and then went to the computer to look up what that little garbage can in the bathroom was for. She was instantly relieved when she found out what it was.

We got into the car for our second appointment with the psychiatrist and we talked about how worry, which she and Dr. G had named "Voldemort" (from *Harry Potter*) made her blow everything out of proportion. I taught her the term *making a mountain out of a molehill* and she understood how she was making things worse than they actually were.

She met with the psychiatrist first and told her all of the horrible things that we were making her do. She also told her how she had talked about killing herself and she basically won over the psychiatrist in a matter of 20 minutes and got her to believe that she was being pushed too much.

I was called into the room and they both convinced me that this approach was too hard for her right now. We sent my daughter out of the room and we decided to offer her the option of returning to school the next day instead of going to the clinic. I had a sense of relief since she begged me the other day to stop this therapy and told me she would go to school like a normal kid. I was so sure she was going to answer yes and would finally go to school and pretend to be normal until the stronger prescription of medication we were getting today would kick in.

I also told the psychiatrist how the clinic threatened to call Child Protection Services. She was very understanding of why I had lost my temper and she said that their accusations were absurd and they were just protecting their jobs. She calmed my fears and told me it would all be fine.

When my daughter came back in the room we offered her the choices and she said, "No!" She said she was never going back to school again and chose to keep going to therapy instead. The psychiatrist explained to her that she would be returning to school the following Monday anyway since therapy would not be everyday starting that week and there was no way around it. She told her she could either go back tomorrow or Monday and those were the only two options. This conversation at least made me able to get her to the clinic the next day since it was her choice.

The next morning during my meeting with Dr. G, I told her about our psychiatry appointment. She explained that my daughter was looking for a weak link. She was looking for anyone or anything that was going to get her out of this. She strongly urged me not to stop the therapy. I agreed to keep going, but I explained that I was skeptical. This was all getting really bad and out of control and I could not see how or when or if this was even going to work.

After I left, their day began with visiting bathrooms again, looking at vomit photos, and also talking with a man in the building that had a gagging cough. Dr. G was great at setting up these exposures. This man was actually another therapist that worked at the clinic. My daughter had to answer questions about him such as how old he was, or if he had any kids, etc. Every time she got an answer wrong, she had to take a step closer to him.

We met again at the end of the day so my daughter could tell me what they did. Thankfully she was less mad that day since she knew it was her choice to go to the clinic instead of to school.

Exposure to Vomit

My daughter and I arrived the next morning for what was supposed to be another three hour session. Dr. G told me that the director of the clinic wanted to meet with me around lunch time so that she could talk to me more about the therapy and what to expect as far as seeing any improvements.

I arrived for the meeting and planned on taking my daughter home afterwards so we could go pick up my son from preschool. The director took me upstairs to her office and she told me that she had just finished setting up vomit in a bathroom stall that my daughter was about to be unknowingly exposed to downstairs with Dr. G.

My eyes opened wide and my heart jumped into my throat. I was scared and curious how that was going to play out. We had a nice conversation about how she has done this therapy many times in the past and that it really works. She explained how it can take longer in kids that are so young, but it does in fact work. She really made me want to believe in this therapy and I agreed to stay in it until the end.

As we were talking, I noticed her phone was constantly vibrating and I was thinking about how busy she must be. She continued to tell me that the goal for next week was to have my daughter start going back to school in the mornings and then back to the clinic in the afternoons.

When our meeting was just about finished, she finally looked at her phone that had been vibrating ferociously the entire time.

She looked concerned as she realized all those vibrations were texts from Dr. G because my daughter was freaking out downstairs.

Dr. G had walked her into the bathroom where the vomit was set up. When she saw it she pushed Dr. G out of the way and was in the hallway downstairs screaming for me. Screaming like no one had ever heard her scream. She was threatening to hurt herself and was out of control. The director told me to take the back stairs out of the building, go pick up my son, and go home and wait for Dr. G to call me.

I did as I was told, putting all of my trust in them. I waited at home watching TV with my son. I was worried and wanted to call them, but I left it in their hands. I sent Dr. G a text after a couple of hours telling her that my daughter had not eaten anything besides half of a granola bar and she must be hungry. She texted me back to say that my daughter was VERY upset and that she would text me when she was calm.

I was supposed to take her from there at 1:00. It was now 4:00 and Dr. G finally texted me to come back. When I got there with my son, Dr. G and my daughter were in the waiting room talking. My daughter looked awful. She was tired and pale. She gave me a big hug and then stayed in the waiting room while her brother and I went with Dr. G to talk. I set him up in the corner with my iPad and he quietly played.

Dr. G looked exhausted. "Welcome to my world," I said. She told me step by step what happened. In addition to walking her into the bathroom with the vomit, they also worked with a cup full of vomit that was put in the hallway. She was finally able to witness all of the mental and physiological signs that my husband and I had seen in the past, although this was much worse than we had ever witnessed. She told me how my daughter yelled and screamed in the halls for me and once she was able to get her into a room, Dr. G had to sit in a chair against the door and sit on her phone to prevent my daughter from taking it to call me. I couldn't believe that my sweet little girl was trying to escape and trying to grab Dr. G's phone. She explained how they just sat in the room together until it passed and until she was calm. I was in shock that she was that distraught, but was glad that Dr. G was able to see all of that. It's amazing how a fear of something can alter someone's behavior so drastically.

When we finished talking she went to get my daughter. We needed to all meet again in the same room they had been in for the day before we could go home. The room still had the cup of the vomit in the corner and she spotted it. After Dr. G was able to get her near it earlier, she would not come into the room now. The anxiety started again and she was telling me to get out of there. She said it smelled bad. I honestly didn't even smell anything. She begged me to come out so she could talk to me in private. Her voice was getting louder and she was shaking. When I wouldn't come out, she went back to the waiting room by herself.

Dr. G explained to me that now that I was there, my daughter was going to need to get my attention and need me to rescue her. The goal was for us to get her back in the room and sit down and talk about the day and any homework. Dr. G instructed me to go tell her, "When you are ready to come and sit down we will talk and then go home." I was supposed to say nothing more and I was not to respond to any questions.

I followed her directions and when my daughter tried to engage me in conversation, I walked out and headed back to the room. This was my exposure therapy now. She kept coming outside the room and begging me to come out. She yelled, "Do you know what Dr. G is doing to me?!" Dr. G whispered to me to ignore. She did a series of coming and going in the hallway and tried to engage in conversation with me. Dr. G was coaching me on what to say and when. I was instructed to give her one more reminder. I said, "As soon as you come in and sit, we can start the meeting and then go home." Then I had to ignore.

I followed Dr. G's lead and we started playing with my son. We listened to him sing songs from pre-school and were trying to show my daughter that we were going on without her and would wait for as long as we had to.

It took an hour! But it worked. It really worked! Ignoring works! We were the last ones to leave the building that day. I was so glad that I had this coaching because now I knew what I had to do at home, and this was the first time I ever saw it work. I just never gave it long enough.

Dr. G jokingly told me later that she even thought to herself where we would all sleep in the room if it took that long to get her back in. We had our meeting and my daughter talked really quickly about the day so she wouldn't breathe in any vomit germs. She had to go out of the room a few times to breathe. It was very dramatic.

Dr. G told her to talk about the day later with my husband and with our friends who knew what she was going through. We talked about Thanksgiving and also how she would be going to school for a couple of hours on Monday morning before our appointment at the clinic.

We were able to leave on a good note after the meeting and she told me more about her day in the car. I noticed that she was talking differently now. She was not angry. She was actually talking like she felt a bit of accomplishment. I was amazed. I let her shower, wash her hands, and pick out prizes. I also let her know how proud of her I was. She then called Daddy, who was away, and our good friend who we were going to spend Thanksgiving with the next day and she told them all about the day.

We had a good couple of days, with a few bumps and battles here and there and I felt confident in my newly found ignoring skills. I was confident that I now knew what and when and how to say certain things and I could see it working. It was like trying to break down a wild animal before you can train them.

The Tantrum

Thanksgiving weekend was manageable and my husband came home on Saturday. I filled him in on everything I had learned and I showed him my notebook full of notes I had jotted down from a long phone conversation with Dr. G on Friday night. It was so amazing that she would call and check on us! I consolidated about thirty sticky notes, which was all I could find when I was on the phone, into a few pages that I could refer to as reminders or if there was a battle.

My daughter was apprehensive about school on Monday, but knowing she was only staying for a few hours helped her not get too worked up. We talked about what she would tell people at school regarding where she had been. She decided she would tell her close friends the truth and just tell everyone else it was personal.

On Monday, November 26th, we woke up at that dreadful 6:30 school morning time. She was scared and had a stomach ache. She took her medicine and ate a few bites of food. She stayed in the bathroom for a while and as it got closer to needing to leave, I told her I would be in the car waiting. I was hoping this would speed her up.

We drove to school and as usual, her stomach started to hurt even more as we got closer. I told her that I loved her, I was proud of her, and that I would pick her up just before PE class at 11:00. She hated PE, so I figured she should have an easy first day back and skip that class. Our appointment with Dr. G was at 1:00 and my plan was to go home for lunch first.

I picked her up from school and as were driving, she started getting angry and nervous about going to the clinic. A quick thought went through my head that we should not go home, but I didn't know what else to do to kill the time before our appointment. Always listen to your sixth sense!

As soon as we got home she started going crazy. She was yelling that she was not going to the clinic and I could not make her. We should not have come home! She was slamming doors and starting to throw things in her room. She screamed that she hated me and that I was a horrible mother. I was now thinking that conversation, the one about child protective services that I had with Dr. G, may actually have been quite helpful. Now I had to use some serious restraint and some really good parenting skills instead of losing my temper.

My daughter said she was going to lock herself in her room. I told her if she did, I would have to call the police to help me get her to the clinic. I was fully prepared to do so since I was supposed to follow through with whatever I said. I thought, *Oh my god! I have just threatened to call the police on my 11 year old, 56lb child.* This was out of control! She was now throwing chairs in the kitchen. I had no idea what to do so I just let her get it out. I texted Dr. G and asked her what I should do. She was trashing our house and screaming loud enough for the whole neighborhood to hear.

Dr. G was amazing. She went above and beyond and was texting back and forth with me for the next hour coaching me through the situation. Following her instructions, I waited outside for my daughter. When she came out to yell at me more, I locked the front door and told her I would wait in the car. When I got in the car she went around the back of the house and got back inside. I waited in the car hoping she would come back out.

After a while, I went in to use the bathroom and simply reminded her that Dr. G was waiting for us and that I would be in the car. She yelled more, but I ignored her and went back outside. Just like at the clinic on the vomit exposure day, she came to the car to yell and then would go back inside. This went on for about thirty minutes or so. I was trying to keep myself busy in the car. Dr. G was also making sure I was staying calm. She told me to organize my purse or my CD's to keep me busy. The mailman saw me and knocked on the window to give me the mail. Great, something to read!

When my daughter finally came outside she wanted to talk about what Dr. G would do with her that day. I said we could talk as soon as she got in the car. She got in and I immediately started to drive. She reminded me that she left the door unlocked and I told her how I hoped the dogs wouldn't get out. There was no way I was giving her another opportunity to go inside the house.

As I drove, she was screaming at me so loud that I had to squint my eyes. Apparently, she really hated me now and I was the worst mother on the planet. She refused to put her seat belt on because she said she hoped she would get hurt if we crashed. I ignored her and fought back my tears.

Suddenly, the movie *The Exorcist* came to mind. If you have seen the movie, you probably remember the part when the priests are trying to drive out the devil and the devil is talking through the girl saying horrible things and making her hurt herself and them. Take away the green vomit and that was my daughter right now. Thankfully we lived five minutes from the clinic.

I texted Dr. G when we got to the parking garage because she would not get out of the car. "Same routine," she told me. So I got out and waited by the entry door. I was shaking and trying so hard to hold myself together. I hoped Dr. G would come out and help me, but she said I had to do it myself.

My daughter eventually got out and I immediately locked the car. Then I went inside the entry and waited for her. That took another five minutes. When she came through the door, I headed to the hallway outside the waiting room. She was yelling in the hallway and people were clearly interested in the situation. Dr. G told me to go into the waiting room. I said no, because there were people in there and I didn't want to scare them. She reminded me that it couldn't be worse than what she did there the other day.

We made it into the waiting room and there was another mother who saw me struggling to not burst into tears. Her teenage daughter was trying to talk to my daughter and ask her why she was so upset. She wanted no part of any conversation, so she got up and left. The Mom told me to be strong and hang in there. She went through this with her daughter and it would get better.

Dr. G saw my daughter by the office and told her that she would come to get her when she was in the waiting room and calm. I couldn't hold myself together any longer and I texted her to please hurry up.

She finally came to the waiting room and had us follow her to the therapy room. My daughter was behind me and did not see my tears. Dr. G saw them and promptly sent me to the bathroom to gather myself so we could all talk. My daughter took a detour because she did not want to walk past the bathroom she saw the vomit in the other day. So we all went our separate ways and met in the room.

When I went in, they were talking about school and how Dr. G was proud of her for getting to school. Since we were late, they were just going to look at some photos online and do things that would be easier for her and that she had accomplished before. We didn't even talk in detail about the trouble getting there. All she said to my daughter was, "I understand it was really hard for you to get here today."

I let them do their thing and I went to the waiting room and called my husband to let him know we were safely there. People were trying to chat with me and I didn't feel like talking. I was supposed to teach later and I couldn't even function.

I went out to the lobby and sat in the corner, on the floor by the elevators where it was quiet. I called my friend and told her that I was not sure if I would make it in to teach. In addition to being my friend, she is also my boss. She asked if everything was okay and I burst into tears. She gave me a pep talk and I felt a bit better. I hung up and just sat there for a while. I didn't know when the last time I slept through the night was. I had lost five pounds that week from the stress and I was exhausted. I checked my email and gathered my thoughts before getting up and going back to the waiting room.

They finished up and Dr. G talked to me alone. She wanted to make sure I was okay and that I realized what a good job I did. She told me that my daughter would have to clean up the mess at home or have privileges taken away. I realized I had won that battle and I was a tiny bit proud of myself for getting her there. I decided to go teach so I could get out of the house and focus on something else.

I was now keeping score of my battles. Mommy 2; my daughter 0. Or, if you want to start from birth, my daughter 987,654,321; Mommy 2.

The next morning, another battle arose. When I woke her up for school she refused to get up. I calmly told her the goal for the day was to get to school and that I needed her to get ready. She told me her stomach hurt and she was not going. I then gave her two choices. That was another new technique I had learned from Dr. G. Giving her choices, even though she didn't always like them, would help to give her a small sense of control.

The choices were to either get dressed in her school uniform or get dressed for the doctor's office so we could get a doctor's note if she was going to miss school. Of course, she didn't like either option and just wanted to stay in bed. Her dream at that point was to never leave our house, be home schooled, and have no social life. I had read that this is what happens to some emetophobics. They grow up to become agoraphobics who cannot even leave their homes. I was not going to let that happen.

So, here I was in another battle. Her yelling began, in front of my son this time since the plan was to bring her to school and then drop him off. He handled it well since I had already explained things to him in a way that Dr. G had helped me figure out. He understood that his sister had a problem that we were trying to help her with. I related her to a particular little boy in his class that often had tantrums and had a hard time following directions.

He understood what was happening as much as a 4 year old could and just followed my lead. My husband followed my lead as well. I met him in the bedroom a couple of times to remind him, and myself, how we were supposed to react and when to ignore. Remember, I had an entire week of training while he was away and now I had to train him. Using all these techniques and skills really took some careful planning.

While she yelled at me from the chair right next to me, my son and I were on the floor playing a game. I was trying to not be bothered by her in the least bit. We played his favorite game of lining up our plastic soldiers and trying to knock each other's soldiers down with a marble. The last one standing is the winner. Ironically, kind of like my life at that moment. My husband was getting ready to leave for the office when we decided we needed to make a different plan. I called our son's school to see how early he could be dropped off and my husband took him to early care while I dealt with her.

She kept up her yelling saying that normal kids that have a stomach ache don't have to go to school. I told her that since she had missed so much school, we would now have to get a doctor's note every time she was late or absent. I needed to be a good liar at the drop of a hat. The school had been amazing and they didn't need any doctor's note. They knew they would have a note from Dr. G when the time came.

She continued with her tantrum. No throwing things that time, though. I started to give her ultimatums. I would write down a time and told her that if she was not ready by that time, she would lose computer privileges. When she wouldn't comply, I wrote down more times taking away more privileges each time.

She was down for no computer for one week and no TV for that day.

Then I threatened her with no TV at bedtime for two nights. This one meant something to her. She needed that TV to fall asleep. It was the only way she could occupy her mind when this all started two years ago and it was her crutch to get to bed. I gave her a good 20 minutes for that one. I reminded her to watch the clock closely since even 1 minute over would result in the punishment. I told her I would be in my room cleaning and to come and get me when she was ready.

I closed my door and hoped to God she was getting ready so I would not have another battle about the TV if I really had to take it out of her room. I heard her getting ready and I was curious if she was getting ready for school or for the doctor's office. I didn't really care. I just needed to be strong and win.

There was a knock on my door and she was ready in her uniform. I got her to school at 9:30 and left her with her guidance counselor. I did it again! Mommy 3; my daughter 0!

The rest of the day was okay. I was able to get her to the clinic after a few hours of school and they worked on spinning in a chair, running in place, and other sensations that would make her feel uncomfortable. This was to get her used to feeling dizzy and out of breath and sweaty. She needed to be used to all of those feelings and be able to cope with them until they felt like a normal part of life. They also worked on getting closer to a bowl of vomit at the end of the hallway by playing games.

The next day, Wednesday, we were supposed to have a break from the clinic because Dr. G had appointments all day. I was able to get my daughter to school for the whole day.

Dr. G called me in the morning and we decided to come in for just an hour in the late afternoon to have an ice cream party since she got to school three days in a row and was washing her hands less. Dr. G also wanted to keep up the momentum of getting her there.

We arrived at the clinic with ice cream and cupcakes. It was not only a celebration, but a way to get Dr. G to see her eat and work on some exposures with food. My daughter did not want to eat anything, but she agreed to take a few bites. She was so thin at this point. I can remember waking her up for school and seeing every bone in her back through her pajamas.

Dr. G had a great idea and started encouraging my daughter to take a bite from her container of ice cream so they could be "ice cream buddies" and share some germs. Then they did the same thing with the cupcakes. I was so impressed that she did it. And, without washing her hands first! She NEVER ate without washing her hands.

Then Dr. G wanted to do some more spinning and physical activities. My daughter asked if I would do the activities with her, so had fun doing jumping jax and running in place. Dr. G also made us spin in a circle and I quietly spun thinking I am too old for this and I might get queasy. We both survived and we left in a fairly good mood.

That night, after such a good day, another battle arose. After we put our son to bed I took a Benadryl so I could maybe actually sleep and I told my daughter and my husband that I was going to bed early. As soon as my head touched the pillow I heard her loud voice and the garage/office door slamming. Ugh, here we go again. Now it was my husband's turn and I was going to let him try to deal with it before I got involved.

He came to the bedroom to fill me in and I reminded him of what he was supposed to do. Now that she knew she couldn't get anywhere with me, it was time to try Daddy. I let them be for at least half an hour. But when she started screaming I got up and asked her to quiet down so she wouldn't wake up her brother. She got louder and I suddenly remembered that Dr. G said if I told her something like that, she was just going to get louder to get more attention. Ugh. That's okay; I was allowed to mess up under the effects of my Benadryl.

I went back to my room and left her in the garage with my husband. She was punching him in the gut and yelling that she needed to get out of the house and never come back. He took it for a bit and then blocked her hands and told her to stop.

She was now in the yard, at 10:30 pm, yelling that she wanted to run away and go live with another family that wouldn't make her do this therapy. Thankfully our closest neighbor was a psychology student and she actually went through a bit of the same thing when she was my daughter's age. Maybe she wouldn't call the police I hoped.

My daughter then told me that she wanted to say the thing that she was not supposed to say. Yes, the words about killing herself. The words that would make either me, under the effects of Benadryl, or my husband who had had a few glasses of wine, have to drive her to the emergency room. We decided it would be me if needed since I wouldn't get arrested for driving under the influence of allergy medicine.

I reminded her that if she needed to say those words then she should, but, then we would need to go immediately to the emergency room. All I was thinking was please don't say it, please don't say it! I need to go to bed! As her yelling and combativeness continued, I realized that I couldn't listen to her all night. So, I finally told her that if she was not quiet and in her bed in 15 minutes, I would take her to the emergency room anyway because she seemed very unstable.

She climbed into my bed with tears streaming down her cheeks and told me that she felt trapped and out of control and that she didn't know what to do. I told her my rehearsed lines of; "I know this must be hard and we have to hang in there and get through it. We are all working to get you better." She finally calmed down and went to bed. Mommy 4; Daddy 1; our daughter 0.

Morning arrived and my husband dropped our son off at school. I decided to go for a walk and really think about how I was going to wake her up for school and what to do for that next possible battle. I decided to let her sleep in for a bit. That way she couldn't use the excuse that she was too tired from going to bed so late.

I woke her up around nine o'clock and told her that we needed to get to school as soon as possible. I explained to her that I had to be home by 10 because an appliance guy was coming to fix the washing machine. Yes, my washing machine broke that week. In addition to all the craziness, I was running out of clean clothes and there were mountains of laundry in the garage. She very respectfully woke up and quietly got ready. I was shocked.

As we were driving to school she was talking nicely, yet tearfully, about how she wanted a chance to prove to us that she could go to school, stop washing her hands so much, and be a normal kid. She told me that the clinic was too much for her and that she could handle things now. She said she had learned enough from Dr. G to be able to be normal and she wanted to prove it to us. She asked me to call Dr. G and tell her all of this. I said I would try, but I also explained to her that if she was better, she should be able to go to the clinic without any problems or tears, go to school without any issues, and get dressed for PE class, which she had not done for the past two days resulting in two zeros. I didn't ease her fears nor did I give any solutions about making therapy easier. We said our goodbyes at school and I reminded her that I would pick her up soon for her appointment at the clinic.

I drove home thinking about all that she had said. Maybe we should let her prove herself to us. She said if she couldn't we could take her right back to the clinic. Maybe last night had turned her around. I was impressed at the mature way she had spoken to me and I felt like I needed to honor it somehow.

I arrived home and met the appliance guy for my washer. He checked it and informed me that it couldn't be fixed. My eyes welled up with tears and I thought he must think I am a bit nutty. He quickly tried to ease my worries and said that he already left a message for my landlord. I apologized for my tears simply telling him that this was the straw that may break the camel's back. That poor guy seemed a bit nervous that he made a woman cry because he couldn't fix her washer!

I forgot about my mountains of laundry and called Dr. G. I told her we needed to either finish this week gently or give things a break. I told her about our horrible night and how nice my daughter was this morning.

Dr. G started talking in her clear, concise, rational way. She explained that our daughter was not able to get to us anymore by screaming and throwing furniture and threatening to kill herself, so now she was trying the nice approach. I instantly saw her point and felt like the biggest sucker on the planet. We decided to talk more about it with my husband and myself when we got there later for our appointment. She also wanted to touch base with my husband since he was back from a business trip and make sure he understood and felt secure with what she was trying to accomplish with our daughter.

When it was time for our appointment we sat down with Dr. G while our daughter stayed in the waiting room. My husband saw this whole ordeal as just a huge way for our daughter to be in control. Dr. G fully agreed and talked about how this whole therapy was not just about getting her comfortable with vomit and taking care of her phobia, but also about stripping her of her control.

He was finally able to ask questions and get answers since he had not gotten to talk to Dr. G as much as I had. Before she brought our daughter into the room she coached us on how to explain to her that we would be continuing therapy as planned.

We were to tell her that if she wanted to be done with therapy faster, it was all in her hands. She would need to show us that she could accomplish everything Dr. G was doing with her at the clinic and she needed to be better at accomplishing her tasks at home and at school.

Dr. G went to get our daughter while we decided who was going to tell her everything that we rehearsed. I hated having to remember what to say and I was so scared to mess something up that we decided he would do the talking. Dr. G brought her into the room and my husband told her everything that we practiced. She understood that the only way out of this was to get through it. And that she had to get through it in a better way. We all agreed we were continuing therapy and my husband and I left the room so they could do their work.

In addition to the photos and chair spinning that week, they worked with a bowl full of vomit. They stayed in the hallway and played games to get her closer to the bowl. She was able to get about four feet away from it which was a major improvement from having a four hour panic attack last week after seeing the vomit in the bathroom. Dr. G asked us to come and watch her in the hallway as she inched closer to the bowl. She was scared and tearful, but she was doing it. I remember sitting on the floor with Dr. G cheering her on while she was coaching her to get closer. I was happy that things were finally getting a bit better, but I was also sad looking at her shaking in the hallway. She was wearing a skirt that day and her legs were just skin and bones. I realized we had a long way to go, but I knew we were in good hands.

A Breakthrough

Today was Friday and we arrived for our final day of intensive, almost daily therapy. Next week we would be meeting only two days for a total of four hours. I left my daughter there and went home to get my son so my husband could get back to work.

Dr. G called me after a while and told me they were ready for me to come back to the clinic. Instead of going to the waiting room as usual, she told me to go to room 215. My son and I found the room and opened the door. Dr. G and my daughter were sitting at a table that had a bowl of vomit on the opposite side. I was amazed at her calmness as she smiled and talked about their day. I couldn't even believe it! Last week she was throwing Dr. G out of her way and now she was sitting with vomit! We talked about how far she had come and how proud of her we all were.

We got into the car and decided we needed to celebrate. She talked about which prize from the prize box she wanted and I apprehensively said, "Hey! Let's go out for dinner to celebrate!" I didn't know if that was pushing it, but I just threw the idea out there. We had not eaten out in a long time.

She thought about it and was not sure. I let her think it over and told her we could go anywhere she wanted. She decided that she wanted to go to one of our favorite places for Japanese. She said she may not eat anything and asked me not to get mad if she didn't, but that she would try. I promised her that I would be happy if we were just able to get there and sit at a table.

She showered and got dressed up. When we arrived I let her choose whether to sit inside or out. She chose outside and she looked calm and happy. I was so proud and took a photo of her to mark our celebration. She ordered what she used to get there all the time and she ate a good amount. She didn't make any of us try it first, nor did she go to the bathroom to wash her hands first. Was this my kid? It was. I hadn't seen her in a while, but it was.

Since our friends were not able to join us that night, we decided we would do it all over again the next night with them. She chose the same place again. I tried to convince her to try another restaurant, but she was not comfortable with that yet. We celebrated again, she ate a lot, and we had a really fun night. I was so incredibly happy!

An Amazing Day

Sunday, December 2nd, was even more amazing! We needed to be in Miami Beach for a business appointment for my husband, so we decided to turn it into a family adventure. It was a great beach day since it was not too hot or sunny, so I made a picnic lunch with things I knew my daughter was comfortable eating. I packed pasta salad, strawberries and waters.

After letting her sleep in, I woke her up and she was in a bad mood and didn't want to go anywhere. She was excited about our beach plans the night before, but now she was a grump. It was just another one of her tweenage moods that we were becoming all too familiar with. That's okay, we could deal with it. We had learned how to ignore her bad moods and were getting pretty good at it. After she finally got out of bed, I heard her getting extra freezer packs to put into the cooler because she was afraid the food would spoil. I told her we didn't need them, but let her put them anyway.

We got into the car and it took a while for her to get out of her bad mood. When we arrived in Miami Beach we were giving our son lots of love and attention since he was happy as usual. We headed to a little Italian café and she grumpily followed us and we simply ignored her. She didn't want anything at the cafe and we made a point to tell our son he could have whatever he wanted. He ordered a croissant and some juice and just as we are about to pay, she decided on a croissant as well. A little smile broke out inside of me as I realized her desire for some positive attention might be coming.

We sat down and she noticed a woman coughing next to us. She obviously has a cold and looked pretty miserable. My daughter didn't mention anything about it but she was looking at the woman a lot. When we left the café she told me how she noticed there were lots of people with colds lately.

I was so proud of her that she did not need to leave the cafe when the woman coughed. She didn't even ask to wash her hands and was able to have a normal conversation about the woman coughing. I was still not used to this yet and I was shocked each time I witnessed these improvements.

We were in Miami Beach that day to let a cleaning woman in to clean an apartment for the owner. We needed to kill four hours while she was there cleaning so we headed to the beach as planned. It started to get dark and rainy and the kids were excited to get wet. We grabbed our umbrellas and the cooler. It looked like a quick passing rain so we set ourselves up on the beach.

Our daughter had this sudden and wonderful sense of freedom. She was running with her arms out and she played chase with her brother. Remembering how she was supposed to practice her task from Dr. G of spinning and getting dizzy, she started to spin in the sand until she fell down. She kept it up and her brother joined in as well.

I was thinking of how I have dreamed of getting this girl to an amusement park someday. We had been before and she refused to go on any rides for fear of throwing up. I have called her my little old lady for years because she is not very daring and has always been a very cautious child. She gets too hot at the beach, doesn't like to get sandy, won't go on rides at amusement parks, needs to be home in time for bed, and the list goes on.

She was careful even as a baby. She didn't even walk until she was 15 months old! Maybe because it was too scary. I had this little child that was speaking full sentences at 9 months old, yet was too afraid to even climb the stairs or be more than three feet from me. Now she was spinning at the beach, falling in the sand, and getting dirty. I was amazed yet again.

We ate our pasta, without washing hands, had some more fun, and then headed out to check on the condo cleaning situation. On the way back to the car we got a smoothie and I was impressed that she still had not been to the bathroom to wash her hands.

The cleaning woman needed a couple more hours, but we were done hanging around in Miami Beach. Our son was sleepy so we decided to go visit our friend's restaurant which was about 15 minutes away. We got there and left our son sleeping in the shady car with the windows down. We sat at an outdoor table next to the car so we could be right next to him. My husband stayed with our son and I went with my daughter to the bathroom so she could finally wash her hands.

We ordered our favorite dish of octopus with olives and potatoes over arugula. Food is the one thing my daughter had always been pretty daring with. Not for a while, but she was. She loved good Italian food and this is a classic Italian dish. She used to want to be a chef someday and would attend culinary camp in the summers. She even won 2nd place in a Giada DeLaurentiis adult cooking and photo contest a couple of years ago. My daughter's photo of her spaghetti with clams is still on Giada's website. There was a time when she was cooking for us all the time, making a mess and loving it. Now she was only going into the kitchen to check the expiration dates and to make sure everything was clean.

After we ate, we drove back to Miami Beach to finish the condo business. On the way back home, we made a quick stop because my husband needed to drop off some keys to a client. Our daughter got out of the car to go with him and then quickly turned around and got back into the car. She said she changed her mind and wanted to stay with her brother and me.

She quietly stared out her window and after a few minutes asked, "What is that?" She was always asking me about stuff she saw on the sidewalks thinking everything was vomit. Without really looking, and sounding annoyed, I told her I didn't know. Then I took a better look and said, "Wow! That is vomit!" Now I realized why she ran back into the car. What a way to get in some real exposure therapy! I couldn't even believe it and neither could she. My daughter actually thought Dr. G may have followed us and could have set it up!

She studied the vomit from the window like Dr. G had made her do at the clinic. She looked at the color, the texture, and everything about it. As she stared at the vomit on the sidewalk, we actually laughed about the irony that it was even there.

Fourth Week of Therapy

It was now week four and we only had to be at the clinic on Tuesday and Friday for two hours each day. My daughter continued to get to school with less anxiety each day, although she was still really nervous to go to the clinic would cry in the waiting room.

On the way to the clinic from school she asked me if we could stop at home first and I simply said no. Of course, I was thinking, *hell no!* I was not going to make that mistake again. When we got to the clinic she kept asking me why we had to keep going to Dr. G if she had such a great weekend. I explained that being fearful about going to the clinic meant they still had work to do. She understood, yet she was still teary and nervously shook her legs in the waiting room. She got so nervous every time someone walked down the hallway thinking it was Dr. G. I knew when she was coming. I knew what her walk sounded like down the hallway. I knew lots of things about the clinic by now.

Dr. G came to get her and led her away. They did their usual work of trying to get closer to a bowl of vomit and playing games with it. Games like turning her back to it while Dr. G either stirred it in a circle or picked it up with a spoon and let it drop into the bowl. She had to listen and guess what she was doing. They finished up and we headed home to get prizes.

In addition to the regular prizes, we started a new reward system last week to help her start washing her hands less and it was working really well. I gave her play money every morning that I printed from the computer. The first few days we started with $20.00. Every time she washed her hands, she had to pay me $1.00, and showers were $3.00. At bedtime, she could use whatever money was left over to buy something from the prize store that we set up in my room.

She and I had a fun time buying nail polish, earrings, and all sorts of other fun things. There were also coupons I made for five minute back tickles and massages and even one for a sleepover in my bed. Her hands were looking so much better and they were no longer cracked and bleeding. They were red and super dry and felt like crocodile skin, but her skin probably needed a while to heal itself.

On Friday, we headed back to the clinic again and she was not scared that day. She had also been to school two mornings in a row without having a stomach ache. Not only was she not scared, but we were smiling. Smiling and talking and laughing. That was the first time we had ever done that in the clinic waiting room.

Dr. G came in and looked at my daughter. She said, "I see a smile!" Then she looked at me and said, "I see two smiles!" She told me what time to come back and I went home for a little bit. I had such a good feeling and I was beginning to let down my guard and really see how far she had come. Last week she was the girl from *The Exorcist*, and now she was my girl. My love.

I got home and quickly typed up a little thank you note for Dr. G. I told her that she was the reason for the smiles on our faces and how I didn't even have the words to thank her enough for giving me back my daughter, and my life. I also let her know about my blog that I had started. Not because I needed or wanted her to read it, but more because I want her to pass it along to any other mother who may be in this situation.

I felt so alone and unsure of everything we were experiencing during these two years. Not many people care to hear that your kid is afraid of vomit and your entire life is a mess because of it. No one really understood the severity of her phobia and the state of our life. As far as everyone we were in contact with on a daily basis knew, I was "Just fine, thank you." And where the heck do you find another parent with a child like mine? I looked online. There were lots of emetophobics that wanted to chat, but I already knew their story. I wanted another Mom, with our story. I wanted desperately to find someone who possibly went through exposure therapy with their child and could have told me that their child turned into the devil, too, and now they were fine.

Dr. G and the clinic director obviously tried to ease my fears and told me that everything that was happening was normal with this type of therapy. Surely they have seen it plenty of times, but it was just not the same. They don't have to go home with these kids.

I went back to get my daughter from the clinic and handed Dr. G my note to read on her own time. They showed me a game of vomit baseball which somehow entailed splattering vomit on the table with a spoon and making a game out of it. Dr. G was great with her array of vomit games.

I know, I know. You are probably thinking, *Ewe! That's disgusting,* and that you would not be able to do that. Well, you would be able to do it if someone forced you. You wouldn't like it, but you wouldn't have a full blown panic attack. That's the difference. I can't tell you how many times I tell someone about my daughter and they respond by telling me they hate throwing up, too. When I try to explain more they just don't seem to understand the severity.

Her homework tasks for the next few days were to take away one hand washing after she used the bathroom at home, start eating more, continue chair spinning, and visit a fast food restaurant. She definitely did not like the fast food task.

Dr. G also mentioned that eventually the same restaurant where my daughter got the food poisoning would have to be our destination. She even offered to be the one to go with her when the time would come.

My daughter was not happy on the way home. She said that Dr. G couldn't make her eat fast food and she was not doing it. I just listened and let her get her frustration out. I already knew my plan about hitting Wendy's in a few days when she calmed down. She would not be able to turn down a chocolate frosty.

More Progress and the School Dance

Another week had passed and it was now Friday, December 14th. We went to a couple of fast food restaurants for french fries and chocolate shakes, and we had burgers from our local burger joint. My daughter finally gained a few pounds and was starting to look better and more energetic.

Her middle school had a Winter Show this week in the gym and it was so nice to be there and see her comfortable in a crowded place without having to cover her face or hold her breath. She went off with her friends after the show and I talked with some of her teachers and thanked them again for all of their patience and kindness. They were amazing during all of this. They kept in touch with us via email and would meet with her to help her get caught up during her free periods.

Her English teacher sat with her one day during study period to help her with a big essay that was for both English and World History that was due two weeks ago. She helped her lay out a plan of typing up her draft and emailing it to her for corrections that weekend. After she corrected it, she would email it back so she could finish it and hand it in on Monday. She also sent me an email saying I could email her that weekend with any questions we had about the essay. I had never heard of a teacher doing this for a student on a weekend.

I was so happy with her school and I cannot even imagine the problems we would have had if she had been in our local public school. They would have flunked her for sure and she would have probably needed to repeat sixth grade with the amount of absences she had. Instead, she finished that quarter with all A's and B's, and it looked like she would finish this quarter the same way. I promised her an iPhone if she did well. Not that I cared too much about her grades right then, but I was amazed that she had done so well considering all that she was going through and I thought she deserved something special.

This Friday night was the Middle School Winter Dance. We had an appointment with Dr. G at 3:00 and then we planned to go to her friend's house where they were all going to get ready together for the dance.

Last night we went last minute shopping for a dress because she realized that she did not like what she had previously decided to wear and was a bit bummed out since she found out that her friends were going to wear some pretty fancy dresses. Normally, I would never run out to the mall at 8 pm because my child is having a fashion crisis, but I decided she deserved to feel good about herself and I wanted to help her fit in with her friends. So off to the mall we went. Thankfully, we found lots of beautiful dresses and shoes right away. Thankfully, because I really hate shopping and I was tired from teaching. We had some girly fun in the dressing room giggling and making sure she could dance in each dress she tried on.

We headed home and suddenly we both had a stomach ache and I thought, *Oh No!* A woman at the ballet school where I teach just told me how she was throwing up for two days with the stomach flu. All I could think was, *No! Don't let this happen!*

My daughter thought that it was some Dr. G plan to get her to throw up. She knew that they cure some emetophobics that way. I eased her fears and said we would never do that. I jokingly told her that if we did come up with some evil scheme, we certainly wouldn't do it the night before the middle school dance. Luckily, our stomach aches subsided and we went to bed just fine.

It was now Friday morning, Decenber 14th. My daughter and her friends all started texting each other as soon as they woke up. They were talking about the dance and reminding each other of what to bring to get ready all together. I loved it! She was in a good mood which made my morning easier. She may have inherited the anxiety from my husband's side, but I get all the credit for the morning grump.

During that day at school she called me twice. Whenever I saw the school's number appear on my phone, my heart would skip a beat. It took me a good year before I stopped answering with fear. I became way too familiar with those calls begging me to pick her up or from the counselor letting me know that she was in her office in tears. I much preferred this day's call; "Mommy, don't forget to pack my nail polish and my shorts for under my dress."

 Our 3:00 session with Dr. G went well. They had not seen each other in a whole week, so it took longer for her to get her tasks done. She was more nervous than the last time, but she was not crying or shaking like before.

She was supposed to get as close to the bowl of vomit as she had previously done, but it took a while. Dr. G explained that it was normal since they were not meeting as frequently. She pointed out to her that when you do something that you are scared of very often, it becomes less fearful. Now that it had been a whole week, it was not as easy. She explained this whole reasoning to her and why we did three weeks of exposure therapy almost every day and how comfortable with her fear she had become. Dr. G told her that without this intense therapy, she would not have gotten better. She would certainly not be able to go to the dance, or even to school, and she would still be avoiding her friends, and food, and would still have cracked and bleeding hands.

After Dr. G explained all of this to her, she asked her who she thought was the reason she was getting better. Of course, I was thinking, *YOU! Dr. G!* However, the answer she wanted from her was Mom and Dad. I started to feel a bit sad remembering how she said she hated me and how I was a horrible mother for doing this to her. I knew she never really meant them, but I was not sure if she was resentful of me. I will never forget that tantrum when she was throwing things and screaming that she hated me. We never really talked about any of that after it happened and she never told me she didn't mean to say those things. I think she may have just said she was sorry.

After Dr. G got her to say it was Mom and Dad that brought her to the clinic and Mom and Dad that paid for the clinic and Mom and Dad that wanted her to get help, she asked her if she ever apologized to me. My daughter and I looked at each other and shook our heads sadly. Dr. G said, "Maybe you should write a letter to Mom. And, maybe Dad needs a letter, too."

We made our next appointment for Monday morning at 8:00. It would be our last appointment until after the Holidays since

Dr. G was going away and we would be heading to Italy on Friday to visit my husband's family. We left with our usual homework assignments of washing hands less, spinning while eating, and eating until she is uncomfortably full. Basically, anything that could induce a stomach ache so she could practice coping with the sensations.

After our appointment, we drove to her friend's house where they were waiting for her to get ready for the Winter Dance. I had never met this Mom before and we wound up chatting for a while. The girls were having fun exchanging Christmas presents and my son was playing.

When I sat down with her friend's Mom she told me right away that she made sure my daughter had a clean towel to shower with since her daughter told her that she was a germ freak. I laughed and thanked her. Then I told her why she is a germ freak.

She listened very attentively and then told me how she understood my feelings of hopelessness and worry. When her daughter was six, she had a brain tumor. I was suddenly embarrassed that I had bored her with our fear of vomit story. I even said so. She told me not to undermine our troubles since having a mentally unstable child is not any less trying than having a physically unstable child. We talked more and shared stories and I saw a wonderful strength and understanding in her.

During this whole ordeal, I had always tried to think of people who had much sadder and more difficult things they were going through. My father, who passed away from a terminal illness when I was in my early 20's, would always tell me that was how he got through his days. He would constantly remind himself that somewhere in the world, there was someone in much more pain that needed more help than him. Those words have always stuck with me but are often hard to live by. Every year on my daughter's birthday I am reminded of his words since she was born on the anniversary of his death.

I said my goodbyes to my daughter and her friends and then went home with my son to enjoy a quiet night with my husband. The dance went well, although she was in a horrible mood when she got home. She had had a long day at school, then the clinic, then the dance. She didn't eat much at all and she gets horribly grumpy when she doesn't eat. When she got home she didn't even want to talk and was very rude when I tried to ask what was wrong. I revoked her computer privileges and then I told her how sad I was that I went out of my way to buy her a beautiful dress and shoes and she couldn't even tell me how the night was. I said good night and I went to bed mad and sad.

Before she fell asleep, she wrote me a letter that she gave to me the next morning. It was a beautiful letter in which she apologized for her behavior and also assured me that when she said she hated me all those times, she did not mean it. I thanked her for the letter and gave her a big hug.

Last Appointment of 2012

Monday, December 17th, was our last appointment with Dr. G before the Holidays. It was an early morning appointment and my daughter brought her breakfast granola bar with her. We also brought Dr. G a little Holiday gift of some of our homemade peppermint chocolate chip cookies and a magnet that had my daughter's new favorite quote; *Just when the caterpillar thought the world was over, it became a butterfly.* She thanked us and we talked about what a meaningful quote that was for my daughter.

Today, Dr. G put her own finger in the vomit while my daughter watched and ate her granola bar. They talked about our upcoming trip to Italy and ended the session with a high five. Two high fives actually, because it took my daughter twice to realize she may have slapped Dr. G's hand that had touched the vomit. She suddenly got scared and asked her which hand touched the vomit. Of course, Dr. G simply looked at her and shrugged her shoulders.

Our next appointment was set up for January 8th. We were to keep up with our homework and look for some good exposure opportunities. The airplane was going to be a good one to start with. Ten hours on a plane with lots of people jammed together coughing and sneezing and all using the same bathrooms.

A New Year

Our trip to Italy was wonderful. My daughter and I both turned another year older and she was so excited to be 12. It was her favorite number for some reason. I turned 40, which was not as exciting. Everyone had been asking me if I was dreading the big 4-0. I had no trouble turning 40. I was just happy that I survived 39. Good bye to the crappiest year of my life!

My daughter continued to improve during our trip and she faced many challenges that she would not have been able to face a few months ago. The plane trip was a breeze for her even with all of the coughing and sneezing. On the way home there was even a woman on the airplane that was throwing up. She was a bit nervous and studied this woman every time she walked past us to go throw up in the bathroom. She wondered why she was throwing up but she coped well with it and didn't ask me any questions.

This was not the only throw up incident she faced. Not only did she cope with the vomit we saw on the street on New Year's Day, but she also survived her brother throwing up. He had a cold and because there was so much mucous in him, he gagged and threw up. She knew it was about to happen and got scared and went to another room. Not thinking, I flushed it right down the toilet instead of making her come and look. She asked me later why I didn't let her see it. I told her it was an automatic response for me to flush the toilet and I should have thought to have her come and look.

She handled the situation really well. She was nervous and jittery, but she wanted to know what it looked like and actually wished she had seen it. She wouldn't kiss me goodnight for fear of catching a stomach bug and she kept her distance saying she was not ready for that yet. She was amazed at how calm I was and asked me why I was not scared. I simply explained that her brother was sick and needed my help. If I got sick too, it would pass and we would all be fine. There was nothing we could do about it, so why freak out. I went to bed and left her with her thoughts. She stayed up late reading and fell asleep without being that needy child she was a few months back.

She had learned so many coping skills these past two years, but was never able to apply them. Now, having been so strongly forced to use her skills with Dr. G at the clinic, they were becoming automatic. I can't even believe what we went through to get to this point and I am so happy that we did not back out of the clinic. I will forever remember the tantrums, the trashing of our house and the threats of her wanting to kill herself as I look at how our lives have improved. It's a new year and it's going to be a great one!

Back to the Clinic

We were now home from Italy and it was the night before we had to go back to the clinic. My daughter was not afraid to go anymore. She was still nervous, but not terrified. At that point she just wanted to get past the vomit work because she was disgusted by it. Not scared, but a more normal reaction of disgust.

She was convinced Dr. G was going to make her touch vomit at tomorrow's appointment and she said she was ready for it. She had been thinking about it during our entire trip to Italy. She wanted to do it and get it over with, but first she wanted to practice at home. So that night, she asked me to chew up some dinner and spit it in a bowl so it would look like vomit. I had no problem doing that. We laughed and made it quite silly. I did a great job and she was utterly disgusted at what really looked like vomit. My husband touched it and she got her brother to touch it, too. It took her about 15 minutes, but she finally dipped her finger right in with a little help from me pushing it in. Yay! She decided she needed a prize from the box for that. She picked out some nice electric blue nail polish and we finished the evening together by watching TV and painting her nails.

The next morning was January 8th and I picked up my daughter from school a bit early so we could get to the clinic for the first appointment of the new year. She had convinced herself that today was the day she will have to touch the vomit and she was ready.

Dr. G arrived to the waiting room and asked us both to come with her. We sat down in the room and my daughter told her that she was cured! She told Dr. G about our trip and about all the vomit that we saw and Dr. G joked that she had international connections for setting up vomit. I think my daughter may have believed her a tiny bit.

I had honestly never seen so much random vomit during these past 2 months and it even made my mind wonder how it was possible. There is a quote I had found not long ago that seems to make sense. It says; "Life will give you whatever experience is most needed for the evolution of your consciousness."

After we talked about our trip, Dr. G told my daughter that the container of vomit was in the room somewhere and she wanted her to find it. She hesitantly looked around and found it under the couch. She took it out with shaky hands and put it on the table. Dr. G told her to open the container. She carefully opened it with her jittery hands trying not to spill it. I was thinking that she was going to do as she planned, and just stick her finger right in. Instead, Dr. G picked up a coffee stirring straw and told my daughter to put it into the vomit and put drops of it on my hand. Oh, the things we do for our kids!

She was really hesitant and expressed concern for my health and felt really bad for me. I told her that I didn't care if she put it on me. Although, I was hoping she wouldn't get any of those green spinach looking pieces on me. As she decorated my palm with drops of vomit, Dr. G talked to us about how well my daughter was doing. She explained how her job is to get herself out of a job when a client is all better, but before she could determine that, she needed to make sure that all aspects of my daughter's life were better. She explained about the theory of over correcting a problem to be sure it is fixed, hence the touching of vomit, which is not something a normal person needs to be able to accomplish in life.

Dr. G asked us a lot of questions to make sure that the separation anxiety and the obsessive compulsive behaviors had also gotten better. My daughter was quick to say yes, but I pointed out that she was still washing her hands too much. It was a whole lot less than before, but still too much.

Dr. G could see that I was right just by looking at her hands that were still red and dry. Her weight was also still an issue. She had gotten up to 61 pounds, but was generally hanging out around 60. She was 65.5 pounds before school began in August, which was still too thin for her age. She was eating more and we agreed that it would probably take some time to put that weight back on, but Dr. G asked me to call our doctor that week to find out her ideal weight.

We then talked about the goals she still needed to accomplish for homework. In addition to eating more, washing hands less (including not washing before dinner if we were using utensils), and planning a boat ride; she reminded us that we were eventually going to have to visit the same restaurant that made her sick. She asked my daughter if she thought she was ready for that, and she surprisingly said yes. Then Dr. G asked me if I thought she was ready. I agreed with my daughter and said that I thought she could probably do it. Dr. G offered to be the one to go with us if my daughter thought she would have trouble with the task, but she seemed confident. Dr. G did not want her to fail this one and really made sure my daughter understood that she was not allowed escape once she walked into the restaurant.

Most people I know, myself included, would probably not go back to a restaurant that made you sick, but this was that part about the over correcting theory and really being able to conquer the very thing that had conquered her for the past 2 years.

Dr. G wrote down the homework for us and we made our appointment for next week. She asked me if I had any more thoughts and I simply said that I was just amazed at how well she was doing.

The next day was our appointment with our psychiatrist, who was also amazed at how well my daughter was doing. Remember that about a month ago, she thought that maybe we should stop this therapy because it was too intense. She was now with me in being a true believer in exposure therapy. Our psychiatrist wanted very much to be able to talk with Dr. G, so she asked me for her phone number. She and the director of the clinic had played phone tag for a while about a month before this and they were still unable to get in touch. Our psychiatrist wanted to decrease her medicine in a few months which I was all for, but she wanted to talk more with Dr. G about everything first.

After a phone conversation with my mother about a month or two ago, when I was completely distraught and feeling like I couldn't live like this anymore, she simply said, "It will pass." Someone told her that many years ago when she was going through a rough time, and she always remembered those three simple words. It will pass. I was starting to be a believer myself.

"The Restaurant" Visit

This week was full of more improvements. Guess where we went? Yes, my daughter completed her biggest homework task ever. We couldn't even say the name of this restaurant for the longest time without inducing panic. We went with our good friends to mark this amazing milestone and to make it more fun.

As soon as they gave out the kid's menus and crayons, my daughter grabbed the red one from her brother. Apparently, the orange or the yellow that were next to her were not good enough to make a huge X over the chicken nuggets. She really needed that red crayon since that is the food she ate the night of the food poisoning.

After violently Xing out the nuggets, she ordered eggs and pancakes that came with bacon and sausage. She did not touch the meat since she is super against fast food meat and the way they treat the animals. I couldn't argue with her about that, so I ate the bacon. She ate two out of the three pancakes and a couple bites of the eggs. I knew the goal was to not to have to eat everything on her plate and I was just proud that she was able to get there, order something, and cope. When we arrived, she said her anxiety was a five. By the time we left it was down to a one.

Before we went to the restaurant, my daughter and I had a girl's only trip to the movies. It was our homework from the psychiatrist. She wanted my daughter to see the movie *Life of Pi*. I had never read the book, but I had heard a bit about the story in the past. After our psychiatrist told us to go and see it, she cringed for a moment and said to me that my daughter may not want to see some of the scenes where the animals are killed by a tiger. Of course my daughter piped right up and said, "That's okay, it's the circle of life." I love my kid. And yes, *The Lion King* was one of our favorite movies when she was little.

I will never forget a school trip to the movies when she was in kindergarten. I accompanied her class to go see a Disney movie called *Eight Below*. In the movie there is a really sad scene in which a sled dog dies. My daughter's little friend looked at her and said something like, "Don't worry, he is just sleeping." My daughter, who was only 4, proceeded to tell her, "Isabella, he is not sleeping, he is dead. It's the circle of life." Isabella had no idea what the heck she was talking about and she wanted to believe he was sleeping. I told my daughter to stop telling her he was dead and to let Isabella think whatever she wanted.

Life of Pi was a visually stunning movie. Although, I didn't realize there was so much of a religious theme in the movie. The whole premise of the movie is how this Indian man is telling his story to a writer about how he found God when he was a young boy shipwrecked on a small boat with a tiger. His struggle to keep the tiger alive yet not get killed by this animal was very symbolic for us.

Since we were there because of the psychiatrist, I saw all sorts of symbolism that was related to my daughter, her phobia, and all that we had been through. They were not the ideas about God and religion that I was probably supposed to draw upon, but I am not a church going woman and I easily found my own interpretation.

At one point in the movie the boy, named Pi, and the tiger are weak and dying from dehydration. After feeding the tiger fish, the boy slowly gains the tiger's trust and in a very poignant scene he sits with the tiger's head on his lap. He cries and tells the tiger, that he has grown to love and that he has worked hard to feed and take care of, that they are dying. During this scene there were tears streaming down my cheeks. This was the moment that really pulled it all together for me. This tiger was just like my daughter's phobia that she had worked so hard to hang onto for the past two years. She had become so close to her phobia a few months before this that I didn't see how her life could get better. It was threatening to kill the girl I knew.

In the next scene of the movie they finally wash ashore and the tiger jumps out of the boat and starts walking towards the forest. The tiger pauses, and Pi desperately wants to say goodbye to him. He expects the tiger to at least turn around and look at him before he heads into the forest, but there is no goodbye or any acknowledgment of the boy whatsoever.

Someday, I will read the book and maybe look for all of the religious symbols, but at that point, I was quite satisfied with my practical interpretation based on my own life. Goodbye Tiger. Goodbye phobia. No need for a sentimental goodbye.

Touching Vomit

Tuesday, January 15th, was our next weekly appointment with Dr. G. A very memorable day since my daughter knew that she was going to be asked to touch vomit. I was pretty sure of it also since we discussed it last week. Dr. G called us all in again like last week and I set up my son to quietly play on the couch while my daughter and I sat with Dr. G at the table.

After we said our hellos, Dr. G told her to search for the vomit which was hidden somewhere in the room again. She found it hiding under a chair and brought it to the table. As Dr. G took the lid off of the container, she looked at my daughter and said, "I thought of you on Sunday." We wondered why for a moment. Then she said to my daughter, "What do you think would make me think of you?" She replied with the obvious "Vomit?" Yes. Dr. G had thrown up on Sunday. My daughter then asked her if the vomit in the container was hers. She confirmed it was not, but told us how she thought about saving some for her. Of course my daughter asked her why she threw up and if anyone else in her family was sick. And, of course, Dr. G reminded her that those were not questions she was going to answer.

We talked about the homework tasks that were accomplished since last week's appointment, with the biggest being our trip to the restaurant that had haunted my daughter for the last two years. Dr. G was thrilled to hear about our successful trip and also the fact that she was not washing her hands before dinner if were using utensils to eat. We talked about the goals we still needed to work on. She was supposed to be eating more and I was supposed to seek out a nutritionist to help her gain weight if it came to that. She still needed to work on washing her hands less, and less vigorously each time.

My daughter washed her hands like a surgeon and the sink was filled with bubbles so much that they oozed out of that extra little drain hole in the sink. I used to take photos of the sink after she was done so that I could show Dr. G when my daughter would try to tell her she was not washing her hands as much.

We also had a long conversation about the medication. During our last visit I had asked Dr. G if she thought she needed to remain on her medication for much longer. She had consulted with the director of the clinic after our last appointment and she strongly advised me to keep her on the medicine for at least another 6 months. Dr. G agreed that she was doing really well and had improved tremendously, but the medicine may have taken the edge off of her anxiety just enough for her to have been able to get through the therapy. She explained in detail to us how exactly the medication helps produce extra levels of serotonin, which her brain may have been lacking.

I listened attentively since I was never a fan of medication. She explained really well that some people need insulin to regulate their blood sugar, some people need glasses to see, and some people need an SSRI medicine to regulate their serotonin. It is not a big dose and the only side effects in her seemed to be heightened happiness and overly good moods at times. I guess I should not have been too concerned.

She also explained that my daughter was in a very vulnerable place. Apparently there is a 50/50 chance of things reoccurring in children with phobias. This was why we were still going to the clinic on a weekly basis and why we should not be changing the medication dosage if things were good. She could have some rough times ahead with school, peers, puberty, and all the other possible pressures of a 12 year old girl. If the medicine can lessen the anxiety and make it all a little smoother, then let it be. She asked me my thoughts and I fully agreed. I was terrified of ever having to go through this ordeal again.

Then, the moment we had all been waiting for arrived. It was time to touch the vomit. The vomit was a lovely shade of yellow today and she was a bit nervous and quite disgusted. It took her a while and we all waited patiently. Dr. G was coaching her about recognizing her thoughts and she was helping her use her detective thinking.

As Dr. G was talking and writing down some notes, my daughter finally dipped her skinny little red over washed finger right into the container, pulled it out quickly, and said, "I did it!" Dr. G told her to do it again since she was writing some notes and conveniently missed it. She did it again and was told to keep it there. I was amazed! While her finger was touching the vomit and they were talking about how she was conquering her fear, who they had previously named Voldemort. I took a picture to mark this moment of truth. Her face tells such a story in that photo. Her smile is gigantic and shows how proud she is of herself, yet her eyes are open so wide because she is so shocked and disgusted that she is actually touching vomit.

She wiped her finger on a tissue and we made next week's appointment. Her brand new iPhone, that she earned today by getting good grades on all of her midterms, was on the table and she asked me to get it for her as we stood up to leave. Of course, I realized it was because she didn't want to get vomit germs on it, so I told her she needed to carry her own phone. Dr. G caught our exchange and gave me a *good job Mom* wink.

We got in the car and I let her clean her finger with a wipe. She showered as soon as we got home and my husband decided we should go out for dinner to celebrate. We had a great time eating out and helping her set up her new phone at dinner.

On the way home one of my all-time favorite songs, "True Colors" by Cindy Lauper, came on the radio. We pulled into the driveway and the song was not over yet so we all stayed in the car. Our daughter was playing on her phone, our son was climbing over the seats, and my husband and I were taking in the song. All I could think of was how happy I was that our family was back. Our fun-loving little family of four was back on track.

ECG Check-up

On Thursday, January 17th, my daughter had an appointment at my doctor's office so they could repeat the ECG that came out abnormal back in November. It is amazing how stress can affect your entire body. After seeing that her left ventricle was enlarged back in November, the doctor had explained to me that it was from her constant anxiety and stress. She had taken me aside on that worrisome day and told me that her phobia needed to be solved ASAP.

Happily, this repeat ECG was completely normal and I was able to cancel the pediatric cardiology appointment that we had scheduled for the next week. I also checked in about my daughter's ideal weight while we were there. I had called last week and the secretary called me back with an answer of 80 lbs. I was kind of shocked since she was only 60 pounds, so I checked again with the doctor. After seeing my daughter and myself and realizing that my husband and I are not very big people, she said another 10 pounds would be sufficient. That was a lot more manageable than trying to put on 20 pounds!

This day was also report card day. I couldn't believe after all that she had been through over the past few months that she was on the honor roll. I was so proud of her. A girl in crisis, who missed weeks of school, was able to just jump in and get right back on track. She was also very excited to learn from her English teacher that she had been invited into the Honors English class for 7th grade.

It was now time to pack for our weekend trip. We were heading to Massachusetts the next day to visit my family. This was the trip we were supposed to take over the Thanksgiving break, but had to cancel in order to begin therapy. There was no chance she would have even gotten on an airplane back then with her fear of germs and people possibly being sick.

I was really looking forward to spending time with my family. I wish we were staying longer so we could visit all of our friends, but that would have to wait until our next trip back. Vacations for the rest of that school year would not involve any missed school days since my daughter had enough absences to last a long time.

Vacation to Massachusetts

The airplane was a breeze for my daughter. We stayed with my parents during our visit and had a wonderful time. We took a few hours out of our visit with my family so that my daughter could have a dose of her two best friends who are twins. It killed me that I was not able to visit more people, but this visit was special for her since shew grew up with these two and missed them a lot. We got a bit sad as we drove by our old house on the way, but we quickly snapped out of it when we arrived at their house.

If what I have read in the past about severe anxiety stunting your growth is true, this was proof. In addition to being the smallest of all her friends here in Miami, the twins now towered over her. She had an amazing time with them and it was wonderful for me to be able to catch up with their Mom who is my very good friend.

While we were at their house, my older sister, whom we had spent the entire previous day with, sent me a text. She was throwing up and had been up all night in the bathroom with what she thought was a stomach bug. What was with all this vomit? I can't believe how much vomit we have seen and the number of people that we know who have thrown up within the past few months. It was really incredible.

Since my daughter is supposed to be exposed to as many germ and vomit situations as possible, I promptly told her that her aunt was sick. She was not too concerned and asked me why she was sick and that was about it. On the way back to my parent's she decided to text her aunt and see how she was and ask her all about it. She wanted to know what it looked like and they had an amusing time texting each other and laughing about the description of the vomit. She had fun reading the texts to me and I was amazed, yet again, at her response and her coping skills. We even saw my sister the next day and my daughter was not scared of her.

It was a great holiday weekend and we flew back to Miami on Monday. We had an appointment with Dr. G on Tuesday and for the first time in a while; there was no work with vomit. Dr. G said she would bring it in occasionally, but weekly work with vomit was done.

My daughter told her about our trip and how my sister was sick. She also told her how she even went to bed one night without having to shower first. That was another big accomplishment. For two years she was not able to go to bed without showering first. I did mention to Dr. G that we were still working on the hand washing and that I was still buying soap way more than I should have been.

Dr. G talked to us about what she would be working on with her for the next weeks of therapy. Since all of the coping skills she learned during the intensive treatment were based on vomit and germs, she now wanted her to learn how to put her "detective thinking" and coping skills towards everything in life such as relationships with friends and family, school, general stress situations, and basically just life in general.

Our appointments were now going to be every other week and then we would taper down to once a month until Dr. G thought the time was right for us to say goodbye. I got a little choked up at the thought of having to say good bye, but I knew the time would come eventually.

I thought this was a fabulous plan since my husband and I had always been dealing with something concerning her. Over the years it had been major separation anxiety, anxiety about friends and school, anxiety about moving, anxiety about allergies and the list goes on. It seemed never ending!

We had said on many occasions, "When she is cured of this vomit phobia, what will be next?" Unfortunately, that was how we had been thinking of her for quite a while. Now she was hopefully going to be able to learn how to deal with any situation that may arise, with a different approach other than anxiety and fear. And we, learning so much as parents over these past few months, would also have better skills to help her.

A New Passion and Continued Success

Back in November, I had seen a coupon for horseback riding lessons. It was just after a friend had been telling me about equine therapy and how horses were being used to heal people from stress and anxiety. I bought the coupon package and hung onto it until I thought the time was right. My daughter has always loved horses and had asked me in the past if she could ride someday. I knew I had to wait until she was comfortable being around germs and animals and I felt like the time had arrived.

When I surprised her with the coupon, she was very skeptical. I had to talk her into going to the barn with me to check it out. She finally agreed, but said she was not going to ride a horse. She told me she only wanted to brush and pet them. She changed her mind when we got there and to this day, is still riding horses.

Not long after starting horseback riding, she decided that she also wanted to try ballet classes again. I knew ballet was not her passion right now even though she was a beautiful dancer. After trying a few classes, she decided it was not for her anymore. I was a bit sad, but was thankful she had found something else that she loved.

It was now May and the school year was coming to an end. She was inducted into the National Junior Honor Society, her health continued to improve, and she had gained 13 pounds since January. I couldn't believe how underweight she had been. I remember seeing every bone in her body not too long ago and even putting on these 13 pounds, she was still under the 50% mark for her age.

We were down to just once a month at the clinic with Dr. G and would probably be saying goodbye to her soon. It was going to be a hard goodbye for me. This woman has saved my child and ultimately our whole family and I felt a great attachment and gratitude towards her. She saw my daughter and myself at our worst and had really been the one to turn our lives around.

Our psychiatrist talked with us about going down to half of her usual dosage of sertraline in the next few months or so. The plan was to have her fully off of her medicine by November of 2013 which would be a year from when she started. This made me a bit nervous for fear of any signs of her phobia or OCD coming back. Dr. G had told us in the past that there is a 50/50 chance of it coming back someday. However, she also reminded me if it did ever come back, we knew where and how to get help.

A Bittersweet Goodbye

Sixth grade ended in late May and Dr. G and I decided we would check back in late July or August after our summer vacation to make sure my daughter was still doing well. If all was well, it would be time to say goodbye. I agreed, although I choked back a lump in my throat at the mention of having to say goodbye.

In the meantime, we spent a really wonderful month in Utila, Honduras, our island destination and our home away from home for the past 7 years. It was such a difficult place to go with my daughter for the past few years. With boat rides, food that needs to be chosen more carefully, fruits and veggies that need to be washed with the utmost of care, and lots of other things that can terrify an emetophobic.

We had a great time visiting with our friends that live there and we met some new amazing people. We went on our little boat often and went horseback riding through the jungle and along the beach. We jumped off the docks to snorkel and we found new creative ways to fight the boredom that can creep in when you are on an island that is only three by seven miles.

During an unforgettable dinner one night, I had an experience that I had never had before. I had this incredible feeling of enlightenment and living in the moment. We travelled by boat with three other couples to a secluded and barely touched section of the island to have a French dinner on the beach.

When we arrived to this French chef's little solar powered home, we were greeted by his bulldog. We drank wine by the fire pit and sat down to an incredible dinner under the moon with the sound of the waves right next to us. While sitting next to the love of my life, and sharing dinner with amazing friends both new and old from around the world, the feeling hit me. We had all talked about our lives and shared stories and history.

One couple was one their honeymoon and her jaw was wired shut since she was in a bicycle accident right before their wedding. Another couple was there for a relaxing vacation. Her boyfriend was a doctor and she was a psychologist at a University. Needless to say, we had lots to talk about. There were also our good friends, who live on the island, who were having a very traumatic week coping with the loss of their friend on the island that killed himself. I also knew this man from our many trips to the island and it was so sad that he left his wife and two children behind.

Conversations went on and I was quietly taking it all in. I thought about that poor man who was so desperate that he thought the only way out was to kill himself and I thought about our past couple of years and how thankful I was that we were here and that our daughter was healing.

Just then, our friend John whispered in my ear and said just what I was thinking. How lucky are we to be sitting here under the moonlight, in this unspoiled piece of nature, with people from various parts of the world sharing stories of life, death, happiness, and struggle. Tears of joy and beauty and accomplishment started to trickle down my cheeks and I couldn't stop them. Everyone started to ask if I was okay. I was! I felt alive and at peace, and suddenly in that moment, all was right and beautiful.

A few days after we came back home to Miami we had our appointment to see Dr. G. We talked about our trip and how my daughter did really well. We showed off her hands which were looking better from not washing them so much. Dr. G asked us if we were ready to say goodbye and my daughter and I said we thought it was time.

She told us how we had been her most successful clients and that she would never forget us. She told my daughter how proud of her she was for all of her hard work and she thanked me for putting my trust in her and not giving up. Then Dr. G said, "Let's go have an ice cream party!" We met her across the street and had ice cream for lunch.

When it was time to say goodbye, we exchanged hugs in the parking lot. I was choking back tears as I let Dr. G know how grateful I was for her help and for the fact that she had saved my child and our family. I gave her such a tight hug and I wished I would never have to let go. I don't know if you have ever had to say goodbye to someone who has saved your child's life, but it is not an easy task.

I got into the car and we were both tearing up. I gave my daughter a big hug and she sobbed in my arms. I let her know how proud of her I was and we talked about how hard it is to say goodbye to someone that has had such an impact on your life. I felt like maybe she didn't let Dr. G really ever know how she really felt about her. I asked her if she wanted to write her a letter and we could give it to her. She agreed and wrote a beautiful letter with photos when we got home.

I called Dr. G the next day to let her know that my daughter wanted to give her the letter. She told me that the director of the clinic would actually like my daughter and me to come back to the clinic to do a post interview with another clinician so that they can see on paper how she had improved. It would be a mini interview much like the 4 hour evaluation we did the first time we went to the clinic back in October. She made sure they arranged the meeting when she would be there so that we could see her afterwards and give her the letter.

The next week we headed back to the clinic for the post therapy interview. My daughter went in first and I was handed a packet of questionnaires to fill out just like back in October. Then we switched and it was my turn to go in while she filled out papers in the waiting room.

As the clinician was asking me all of the same questions as last time about rating her anxiety, depression, and suicidal thoughts, I was trying hard not to cry. I was remembering my answers back in October during the first evaluation. I was so overwhelmed with gratitude and amazement at how different my answers were this time. I didn't show my emotions and I managed to get through the interview without any tears, until Dr. G came into the room at the end.

Now we really had to say goodbye. All over again! Dr. G met with my daughter first so they could read the letter together. When they called me back in we talked about how hard it was to say goodbye. I tearfully told her that I couldn't imagine where we would be without her help. We hugged again, I cried some more, and we left the clinic. The clinic, and the psychologist, that saved my beautiful child and my family.

As hard as it was to leave, I hoped we would never need their help again. It was a bittersweet goodbye.

Ebola

7th grade went by without a hitch. She continued to gain weight slowly and she was able to discontinue taking the sertraline. In 8th grade she wasn't riding horses as much since she joined the dance team at her school and she started ballet classes again. Her phobia had not returned for the most part, but it did try to creep its way back in.

When the news broke about Ebola in October of 2014, I got a bit worried. My daughter is supposed to live an exposure life; meaning we are not supposed to be shielding her from things related to illness and vomit. However, I was really scared this one could bring back her phobia since one of the main symptoms of Ebola is severe vomiting. Talk of Ebola was all over the TV news channels so I stopped putting the news on when she was home and I decided to avoid mentioning anything. I would just let her figure this one out for herself and wait for her to come to me.

Of course, it didn't take long for her to figure it out. Her school required every student to have a tablet since all their textbooks are online as well as their homework and school work. What I didn't plan for was the fact that every time she opened her tablet and went online the news pops up. Right there in her face, at 8:00 every school morning, she would get a dose of the headlines. It's pretty hard to shield a teenager from anything these days.

I can remember being young and watching the news with my parents. There would be an occasional missing child, or a fire, or a deadly car accident. All reminders for me that I should not talk to strangers, know how to call 911, and remember to wear my seat belt. These days I was having to make sure I put the TV on a cartoon channel when I went to bed, so that when my 6-year-old son woke up before me and turned on the TV, he would not see people being beheaded by men with black masks or seeing school children blown up or shot to death.

As soon as my daughter found out about Ebola at school, she began asking me questions. I would answer her very nonchalantly so that she would see that I was not concerned. She couldn't get me to join in and be worried with her, but her friends at school were all the fuel she needed. Everyone was talking about it and she would come home from school and give me the latest on who had Ebola and what hospital they were being treated at.

She had concerns about Dallas being not that far from Miami since there was a man that died there, as well as the two nurses that contracted Ebola from him. She was starting to wash her hands more and was checking where the foods in our house were grown, manufactured, and packaged. She would not eat anything that had Texas typed anywhere on the label. There was a lot of food from Texas I learned.

I decided that it might be a good time to check in with the CAMAT clinic. I knew Dr. G had moved away and I didn't want to go through the whole story with someone who did not know us, so I called the director. She gave me some good ideas and some things to explain to my daughter about how the media does an excellent job of blowing things out of proportion. My daughter understood that she needed to base any fears on facts, and that there were no facts right now to support her fear of contracting Ebola. She still continued to bombard me with questions every day and I would simply reply that I was not concerned and that I would let her know if we needed to be concerned.

As the Ebola news started to fade, so did her questions. I was relieved that her fears died back down. However, I did notice she was still washing her hands a bit more than her usual amount, which is already more than most people. I also noticed she was starting to not want to eat out much and she was limiting her restaurant food choices. Depending on the type of restaurant, it was either french fries and lemonade, or miso soup and white rice.

It took me a little bit to realize this needed our attention until my husband and my friend pointed it out to me. When you have a child like this, I feel like there are certain things that you allow. For instance, I know she will always be a person that washes her hands more than others and that she will always be more aware if there are illnesses going around. I found myself allowing these things until I realized I was buying soap way more often than I should have been, I was suddenly being asked to sniff milk again (because she thinks it's old), and I was being told by her to wash my hands.

So back to the clinic we went. Thankfully, all it took was a couple of visits with the director to get back on track. Most of the worrisome signs went away as soon as the director explained to my daughter that if she can't control her hand washing and avoidance of foods with us at home, then she will have to work on them at the clinic. She never wants to do that again and neither do I unless it's a last resort.

The director told us that our daughter could definitely use some more sessions with her to help with the hand washing and avoidance of foods, but I opted for us trying things at home first under her guidance. I do not want to deal with my daughter hating me again and turning our lives upside down.

Our homework was to eat out a lot and eat a variety of things when we go out. We made a list of things with the director that my daughter needed to be able to order. We started with the easy ones and worked our way up to things that scared her such as meat. She had no problem eating meat at home but, eating it out where she can't control the buying and the cooking was hard for her. She had been gluten free for about a year which solved some stomach issues she was having. Being gluten free was already limiting her choices, so she really needed to be flexible when she was not at home and be able to eat things like meat and fish.

After a few months of working on these things she was doing well again. We continued to check in with the director every two months which helped to keep my daughter on track. She knows that her lifelong goal is to be continuously aware of her thoughts and actions and to remember the skills she has learned so she does not fall back into safety behaviors and fear.

As her parents, it is our job to make sure she is using these skills now so that when she goes off to college, or wherever she may end up, she will be in control. Right now she has my husband and I making sure she is ordering what she needs to at restaurants and reminding her to not wash her hands too much.

The ultimate goal is to have *her* be in charge of what she needs to order and to have *her* remind herself about not washing her hands too much.

In the News

Every month or so I was receiving emails from parents that would find my blog. Sometimes I would also hear from adults that have thought about exposure therapy for themselves but need some encouragement to try it. It saddens me to hear from some families that have tried to find help for their children and are unable to. There are not many psychologists or clinics that offer such intense therapy.

I met one family that was able to come to Miami to the CAMAT program after reading my blog and talking with me. Their son, who is the same age as my daughter, had seen many psychologists who were unable to help him, and there were no other options in their city. They couldn't even find a clinic willing to do exposure therapy with a child. They had some success here, but unfortunately their son had other underlying health issues that complicated his health.

I have also been able to point a few families in the right direction to get help for their children in other states. Mostly what I hear from these mothers who find my blog is a relief that they are not alone.

In March of 2014, we received a call from Dr. G and the director of the clinic asking us if we would be willing to share our story with the *Miami Herald*. The newspaper was doing a story on the CAMAT program and they wanted to talk with a family that had been successfully helped by them. When I told my daughter about this, she thought it was cool. It was her choice to go ahead with it and it was her choice to allow our names to be used.

A reporter and a photographer came to our home and interviewed my daughter and me. On Tuesday, March 25th, my daughter's photo and story were on the cover of the Tropical Life section of the *Miami Herald*. The article was titled *When a Child's Anxieties Take Over*. I loved the title since it really seemed to encompass our life. This was how I decided on the name of this book. I tweaked it a little obviously since I couldn't copy the title. The article talked about other generalized anxieties as well which is why I changed anxieties to anxiety.

The response was wonderful. I was in a hotel with a friend of mine in the Florida Keys on the day the article came out in the Herald. We were sitting by the pool and there was a man reading the paper directly across from me on the other side of the pool. It was so strange because the story began on the cover with a big photo of my daughter and he was just sitting in his lounge chair reading the inside with my daughter's photo towards me. I walked over to him after a while and told him that's my daughter. He had read the story and was so kind and thankful. He told me about a friend of his who had a child with some other anxiety issues and he was going to share the paper with them.

Some of my ballet student's families who saw the story were amazed by our story. They had no idea we had gone through any of this. My daughter's school displayed the article in the faculty lounge and I heard from many teachers and administrators that were touched by our story. Dr. J told me not too long ago that after the story came out there were a few families that travelled to Miami from other states to get help from the clinic.

I hesitated about writing this book. Hesitated because I know there are so many other books about personal struggles, physical illness and death, and other things that are much more well-known and talked about. However, when I would contemplate giving up on this book idea, I would think about how mental health issues seem to be put on the back burner and are often stigmatized.

I want people to know about the struggle that families go through with mental illness. The emotional, physical, and financial struggle can be overwhelming and the right help is not always easy to find. None of the help we received was covered by any insurance and I am so thankful we were able to afford psychologists, a psychiatrist, and medication. I often wonder about the number of people who struggle in silence because they cannot afford help.

Relapse

It's now July of 2018 as I write this second edition of my book. We have found out that sometimes this phobia can creep back in and it seems more like a lifelong battle. We were warned by Dr. G that there was a 50/50 chance of it returning, and here we are again.

It's not like curing a fear of heights or spiders or flying or really anything else. People with most fears can avoid them. One can take the stairs instead of an elevator or drive instead of fly. For an emetophobic, they can't escape themselves. Every bodily sensation provokes fear or at least an alert. The anxiety is prompted by anything that might lead to vomiting. A headache, a stomach ache, or even a stomach noise turns into fear. The horrible irony is that anxiety causes stomach distress which in turn evokes more anxiety. The belief that these sensations (or the actual act of throwing up) are a serious threat is what leads to the tipping point. This is a phobia. This is emetophobia.

Unfortunately, my daughter, who is now 17, has had a couple relapses. Nothing has compared to when she was 11 and 12 years old, but she has been struggling again for about a year or so. Her phobia was pretty much nonexistent for a year and half after she finished exposure therapy until she threw up towards the end of 8th grade. Thankfully, because of the exposure therapy she has been through, she didn't revert to what we went through after the initial food poisoning that spiraled her life out of control.

She never figured out why she threw up this last time. Maybe it was something she ate or maybe she had a virus. For my daughter, this was very important so she would be able to avoid whatever made her sick and be able to have that false sense of control that she could do something to avoid throwing up again.

When she threw up, we all looked at each other in shock and she actually laughed. She had a sudden realization that it wasn't that bad. All that worrying in previous years for this? My husband and I were in total amazement at the fact that she wasn't freaking out. For years, we all had this built up anticipation of what would happen when she throws up again and here it was finally happening! Sadly, she threw up all night and her initial feelings of it not being so bad were taken over by misery and fear.

After about 6 months of trying to handle her fears ourselves, I reached out to Dr. J and she agreed we should see her for a bit to help things get back under control. My daughter was finishing 9th grade and was back into her fear habits of checking expiration dates and not wanting to go out to eat. I took her to a gastroenterologist because of her constant stomach pains and she was diagnosed with IBS. The doctor didn't really offer much advice aside from handling her anxiety.

My daughter was also begging me to let her become vegan for a long time. She has always been very passionate about animals, but I also know that she believes being vegan would help cut out a whole lot of food safety issues. I told her that once she could prove that she can get things under control with Dr. J then I will consider letting her become vegan.

On the way to Dr. J's office each week, I would have to go pick up some takeout food from random restaurants that my daughter has never nor would ever choose to eat from. They would work on exposures around the food such as sharing utensils and even eating off the desk or eating something that fell (purposely) onto the floor. Simply eating food that was from a restaurant she didn't know or trust was a feat in itself.

After having sessions in Dr. J's office for a couple of months, we moved on to meeting Dr. J at other places. We met at Target once where the two of them went shopping for expired or close to expired foods and then they worked on eating them at the dining section of Target. We also had a few sessions at our house to help her work on eating at home. She doesn't like to eat things that I cook, and especially that my husband cooks, since she doesn't trust how we wash our hands or prepare things. She is constantly reading up on food safety and is always on alert.

We stopped seeing Dr. J after a few months since her schedule was getting busy and things were going much better. My daughter was also about to go away for a few weeks to a ballet summer intensive. Her first time ever going away without me! As a ballet dancer, students her age and level should be auditioning for summer ballet programs. Since I was a ballerina and I am one of her teachers, I am quite involved in her ballet training.

Our ballet studio makes it mandatory that all dancers of a certain age audition for these summer intensives. They don't have to go to one, but they must audition for at least three places to gain audition experience. She was a tad resistant to auditioning since she didn't want to go away. I assumed she would never agree to go away to one of these programs since she would have to leave the safety of home, but when auditions began, I saw her excitement when she was getting accepted into some prestigious ballet programs. She and her friends started contemplating about where they would go for the summer and I was so happy to see this. Along with a few of her ballet friends, she chose the Nutmeg Conservatory in CT. I was so excited for her and so happy that her fear was not stopping her. So, in the summer before 10th grade, she stayed away from home without me for the first time ever. She called me every day because she was scared when others didn't feel well or if she had a headache or stomach ache. She lost some weight since eating outside of home was still not that easy, but I didn't care since she accomplished something I never thought possible!

Current Relapse/IBS

The next relapse, the one we are still dealing with, began towards the end of 10th grade and reared its ugly face during the start of 11th grade in 2017. Her phobia didn't go away after her early summer therapy with Dr. J in 2016. I didn't expect it to since we were not doing the same kind of intensive treatment we had done in the past. Being much older, there was no way I could force her into that kind of therapy again. She just needed to learn how to cope with some of her actions surrounding the phobia, but the phobia still lingered.

After she threw up that last time, her brain decided that she would never let her guard down again and that she needed to be on constant alert. It kind of makes sense in her world of anxiety. It's totally not logical, but when you think about it from her point of view, you can see the connection. She was basically cured after her initial exposure therapy back when she was 13 and she stopped worrying about throwing up. She stopped taking precautions like washing her hands obsessively and checking expiration dates. And then... she threw up. Obviously, it was bound to happen at some point and not because she was not on alert anymore, but unfortunately, her brain made the wrong connection and now she is stuck.

I believe things started getting out of hand with the stress of school which simply added to her phobia that was ever so slowly creeping back in over the past few years. I am imagining it like a termite. You find a few dead ones here and there and slowly you start cleaning up more and more. After a few months you finally go pull out a ladder to climb up into the attic and boom - they are everywhere! They have been quietly eating the house from the inside out and now you need a plan to get rid of them fast and repair the damage. If only there was some spray for this damn phobia. Simply kill it and rebuild.

Towards the end of 10th grade, her stomach started to bother her more and more. It also didn't help her fears when a 48 hour stomach bug made its way from my son, to me and then to my husband. As soon as she found out her brother was sick, she stayed far away from him. She asked me tons of questions but was handling it pretty well until the next night when I started throwing up. She locked herself in her bedroom and screamed and cried. My husband tried to console her via cell phone since she wouldn't open her door. She has a big room with her own bathroom which made it easy for her to stay holed up in there for as long as she wanted. I was fine the next day and then my husband got sick late that night. We kept it a secret from her when he got sick since I thought it would completely throw her over the edge. Maybe if she thought he was fine, she would have some hope that she was not the final one in the house to be doomed. She stayed out of the kitchen and away from us for 10 days, which is the amount of time google told her that the germs can hang around. Luckily, or unluckily, she never got sick. She survived on Luna bars, which she had in her bedroom, and her school lunches. I say unluckily because the fact that she kept her distance and didn't get sick solidified that her avoidance and phobia does in fact keep her safe.

She continued to have the IBS constipation and diarrhea and stomach pains every day for the remainder of 10th grade. I knew it was her anxiety making things worse along with the academic and social stress from school. Imagine an emetophobic with IBS... Her stomach hurts, she gets anxiety because she is afraid she will throw up, the anxiety makes the IBS worse, which then makes the phobia worse, which then makes the IBS worse. It's a circle of hell!

She started missing some days of school towards the end of the school year and we just sort of dealt with it ourselves knowing that school was almost out for the summer and we needed to focus on getting ready for another ballet summer intensive.

She was accepted to attend Walnut Hill School for the Arts in MA which was very exciting and special because it's where I went to high school and where I taught for a few years when she was young. She would be spending a long 5 weeks there. She was nervous but felt a little bit at home since she had grown up only a few miles away from there and was familiar with the school. I lived at this boarding school for two years and was thrilled she was going to get to experience this magical place with it's wonderful ballet training. To make it even more exciting, she was also offered a spot for the 11th grade school year!

This was the hardest decision she has ever had to make and it tore her apart. She wanted to take the 5 weeks and really experience life at Walnut Hill before she made her decision. I tried not to push her one way or the other, although I really thought it would be an amazing growth experience for her and I was hoping she would say yes.

She was stressed out the entire 5 weeks because she was in turmoil. She didn't want to go back to her school in Miami, but she didn't want to live so far from home even though her grandparents and her aunt live only an hour away from the school and promised they would visit her a lot. She called me every day, more than the previous summer, complaining of stomach aches and headaches. We had many discussions about the pros and cons of going to school there in the fall and she finally was leaning towards a yes. It all fell apart though when she went to a meeting for the students that were interested in staying for the school year.

The subject of dorm parent duties came up at the meeting and the woman who was talking was a dorm parent during the school year. She talked about how the students should be at ease knowing that if they ever have a problem or get sick in the middle of the night the dorm parents are always there for them. The conversation morphed into how some years the stomach flu goes through the dorms! I am sure you have figured out now that her yes, turned into a no. Absolutely not. No way. Not happening. Get me out of here now.

We talked and talked and talked for the next week as the decision deadline was coming up. I left a message for her psychiatrist to get her opinion, but she was on vacation. After much contemplating, she decided she could commit to going and trying it for a few months, but only if she could have her own room. The school tried their hardest to accommodate her single room request, but the last spot for the fall was for her, and it was not in a single room. They tried to see if there was anyone they could move around, but they couldn't make it work in our favor. After the decision was made, the psychiatrist called me back and said it was probably for the better. She did not think my daughter would have been able to handle it.

A few weeks after she returned home, 11th grade began. She was very unhappy and depressed. Each week became more of a struggle. She was constantly feeling sick to her stomach and was depressed and stressed out. I reached out again to Dr. J and she agreed it was time for help again. She was not seeing clients anymore because of her schedule at the University. She passed us along to her fellow psychologist at the university and was able to fill her in on my daughter's lengthy history.

We started seeing Dr. A in September of 2017 and we still see her every week. My daughter was starting to have more frequent panic attacks, was very depressed, and we were having a really hard time getting her to go to school. Her stomach was a mess and she was freaking out because it was getting harder to keep up with her classes while missing so much school. She has always been set on getting A's, yet she had no drive to do homework or missing classwork. She was taking all Honors and AP classes and just couldn't keep up since she would be up late at night having stomach aches which would lead to panic and was unable to get any homework done. In the mornings she was so stressed out because she didn't do her homework that she would refuse to go to school. She was missing various honor society meetings in the afternoons and was about to be put on probation for those.

We came up with a rule that if she didn't go to school, she couldn't go to ballet. It worked initially until she started missing too much ballet. She decided life was not worth living anymore if she couldn't dance. Ballet was the only place she felt happy and healthy for the most part and she now wanted to die. Ballet was also where her friends were. She had some friends at school, but not like her ballet friends that she is very close to. Dr. A helped us write up a suicide contract much like the one we had hanging on our fridge back when she was 12. Things were not getting better and our whole family life was suffering. The school offered dropping AP classes and honor societies, but she said no. She didn't want to be seen as a failure or looked down upon by the other students and her teachers.

Dr J, who was still following her progress, suggested we find a new Gastroenterologist since the one we went to previously just sent us away saying it's IBS from her anxiety. She offered no problem solving and no medical intervention and no follow up appointment. Dr J gave us the name of an amazing doctor who did a whole physical work up. She even did a colonoscopy and an endoscopy after a few months of trying things that were not working so that she could rule out any other possible problems. As it turns out, it is in fact IBS, made worse by anxiety along with some intestinal motility issues (basically the rate in which the food moves through her intestines). She had stomach issues when she was young with constipation and diarrhea, so I guess she is just prone to this. And of course, the anxiety doesn't help. She suggested we try hypnotherapy in addition to some medications to help to stop the stomach spams and help her gain weight. She was only about 90 lbs. at this point.

No More School... as we know it

Things started getting pretty bad in October and November and I began looking at other schooling options. We sat down with Dr. J and Dr. A to talk about options and strategies. They really did not want us accommodating the anxiety in any way and they really wanted her to stay in school.

We all agreed that homeschooling was not an option since she would never leave the house and has the personality that could very much lead to her becoming an agoraphobic. I felt like she was going to spiral out of control and wind up in a treatment facility if I didn't find another option. A treatment facility that is four hours away from Miami was an option that they told us to consider. I was very much against it for several reasons. First of all, our insurance does not cover anything like that. I can't even get psychology or psychiatry visits covered. Secondly, it is a non-residential treatment program where they would most likely be doing exposure therapy. I knew there was no way any of us would be able to handle that again. One thing would be to put her in a full-time residential facility where she would have help 24/7, but to do intensive therapy for 4 hours a day and then give her back to me or my husband or whichever one of us agreed to live four hours away temporarily was definitely not feasible. Not after what we went through when she was 11 and 12 years old.

Against Dr. A's and Dr. J's advice, my husband and I decided to pull her out of school after I found another solution. A brand-new school had just opened very close to our house. It's a school that is based on an online curriculum with academic coaches on site. Students make their own schedules and there are teachers there to help with all the courses. Our psychologists were at least hopeful because we were not just pulling her out of school and letting her stay home. I made it pretty clear that I could not handle our home life as is. Having to yell every morning because she won't get out of bed, consoling her at night while she is having panic attacks, and wondering when the moment will come when I must take her to the ER because she wants to kill herself is not the way I want to live. We had to make a change unless we wanted to go down the road of very expensive treatment options that are never guaranteed to work.

In November of 2017, we withdrew her from the school where she had spent the last 5 years. I had so many conflicting feelings about it. It felt wrong, yet it felt right. It felt like we were giving up, but it also felt like we were standing up against the academic system that was feeding into her stress. We made sure that all of us, the new school, Dr. A and my husband and I, came up with a schedule together that my daughter would need to follow. It was also in the plan that Dr. A would have a conversation with the director of the school regarding things that would be helpful and not helpful. The school is quite flexible and the students that were already there basically came and went according to their sports or sleep schedules. My daughter needed more of a solid set in stone schedule or she would wind up staying in bed all day.

They welcomed our daughter as their 4th student and were absolutely helpful and understanding. We agreed on a 10:00-2:00 schedule Monday through Friday. The new school initially alleviated lots of stress and allowed her to be able to deal with her morning IBS issues a bit better. After a month or so, she started to not follow her schedule and there were many mornings that I would still have to be yelling to get her out of bed. She would text me that her stomach hurt and can I please pick her up. I tried hard not to feed into her anxiety and I would ignore her texts for the most part. We still had the no school=no ballet rule. It was only having to be used maybe one day a week initially until it started to become a more frequent thing. She hates school so much that any school at all sucks in her mind. She was totally burnt out from school. She was still overwhelmed with her AP Science class that was transferred over and she was also trying to get used to the online classes without speaking up and asking for help.

After a few months of this she had a breakdown one night. She was under pressure for not completing things on time for her online classes and was unhappy because she was missing ballet classes because of not going to school. On a cool February night at almost midnight, I wound up driving her to the Miami Children's Hospital ER because she was having such a bad panic attack and was saying over and over that she wanted to die. We stayed there for about 4 hours and by the time the doctor came in she was fine and we went home.

I called our psychiatrist the next day and the first appointment she could get us was 4 days away. In the meantime, she gave us a prescription for clonazepam, which is basically a valium, to be used for the short term in case of another panic attack or severe depression. I also called Dr. A who gave me reminders about how to deal with the depression. She was away at a conference but gave me her cell phone number and was very helpful from afar. She made it clear that I needed to try to get her out of bed and be active as much as I could. It is not easy getting a depressed 17-year-old out of bed, but I was able to get her to walk the dogs with me and play some games.

New Psychiatrist

We made it to the appointment with her psychiatrist 4 days later and agreed that her medication needed to be changed. She suggested we get a second psychiatric opinion and had me call a friend of hers who she thought would be more knowledgeable with pediatrics and phobias. I called him and he told me about a different psychiatrist who could probably be more helpful.

I made an appointment with her and she turned out to be wonderful! After we shared the long history, our latest visit to the ER and the medications we have tried, she knew we needed to change things. She told us about a genetic screening that identifies which psychiatric medicines would be best for my daughter's specific genes. We decided to spend the money and get that done instead of just guessing by trying different medications until we find the right one.

The genetic screening came back two days later and was extremely helpful. The medication we had talked about switching to with this new psychiatrist and our last one was in the red category. There are three categories in the report. Green, yellow and red. In the green, we had 4 medications to choose from that were found to interact well with her genes. In the yellow were 5 medications with notes next to each one about why they are not ideal for her genes. Both medications she had been on in the past were listed in the yellow which is why they were probably not very effective. In the red category were 13 drugs listed. The one with the most negative markers was the one we had talked about switching to! Yikes! These are a few of the notes/negative markers so you have an idea; 1. Use of this drug may increase side effects, 2. FDA label identifies a potential gene-drug interaction with this medication, and 3. Genotype may impact drug mechanism of action and result in reduced efficacy.

Another really important thing the test showed was that she has a gene that prevents her body from metabolizing folate into L-methylfolate. Again, there were three categories and her folate conversion was so low that it was in the red. Folate is very important for the brain and people that have this gene are more prone to suffer with mental health issues. It was also explained to me that her lack of folate was and would continue to prevent her body from metabolizing any psychiatric medication properly until we treat that.

The new psychiatrist gave me specific instructions on how to titrate from the current medication to the new one. We basically just needed to slowly lower the dosage of the current med, then add a low dose of the new one after a few days, then stop the old one and then increase the dosage to her current amount. In addition to the new SNRI (instead of an SSRI), she would need to take another pill every day, probably forever, that is simply folate that has already been converted to L-methylfolate so it can automatically be used to create seratonin, norepinephrine and dopamine in the brain. It's not even considered a drug, so my insurance doesn't cover it. It's considered medical food and has no side effects. The psychiatrist told me about an online pharmacy she uses for that drug which cuts the price almost in half.

The psychiatrist explained that both new medicines take about 4-8 weeks to take effect. It was a long 6 weeks after we started to see a difference. I was still having to coerce her into getting out of bed and there were a few instances where I just laid in bed with her while she cried. It's so hard trying to give someone the will to live when all they see is despair.

Much to my surprise, my daughter started looking into hypnotherapy online since the Gastroenterology doctor had mentioned it could help her stomach. I was so excited that she wanted to try it that I found a place in Miami Beach and made an appointment right away. Unfortunately, after a few sessions, I realized it was not going to work. Deep down, she doesn't want to get rid of the phobia since she believes it is keeping her safe from throwing up. It was so exciting initially and we really thought it was going to help. The hypnotherapist was amazing, but my daughter was just not able to buy into it and let her phobia go.

Once I was able to get her back to school we started a new rule which was no school = no phone instead of no ballet. Dr. A and I came up with the plan together after trying to figure out what would motivate her to do the things she is supposed to do. We changed the rule since I know that ballet is the only thing she does that is healthy for her mind and her body and I didn't think we should be taking that away.

We were also able to drop some academic classes that she didn't even need. She was stressing over that AP Environmental Science class which her previous school didn't even tell us she didn't need. She finished all her necessary science credits in 10th grade! After sitting down with the new school director and figuring out how many credits she actually needs to graduate, we were able to drop lots of things, including science, so she only had the 3 core subjects that she needed for 11th grade. Her senior year should be a breeze since she only needs an English and a History class.

This made me realize the insane schedules that a lot of schools are pushing on kids. To be taking 7 classes with tons of homework and tests every day when you really only need half of them is crazy. If you have plans of ivy league schools or a career in science or medicine, then yes, those classes would have been great. I wish high schools were better about giving kids what they need and not overloading them to the point they want to die from the stress. Thinking back, I am not sure why she was made to take honors High School classes in 8th grade. She had impeccable grades so I guess that was just the track in her school if you were one of the "smart kids". I didn't know any better aside from the fact that it didn't feel right to me. I just went along with the schedule since that's what everyone else we knew was doing.

That "smart kid" track led to taking AP classes as soon as high school began in addition to her Honors classes. I am now a believer that this mentality is what is leading to the stress and suicide rates among high school students. Why can't kids in middle school take middle school classes, kids in high school take high school classes and let the college kids take the college classes? My son will start middle school in 2019 and I am taking this all into consideration. He is already in a school that boasts about their accelerated curriculum. Most of his subjects are the curriculum of the next grade up. I have friends with kids in his class that hire tutors to help their kids keep up! Tutors in 4th grade for kids that are stressed and having trouble with the 5th grade math they are being taught is not the path I want. My son earned a B- all on his own with no tutors and not much homework help. A B- is totally unacceptable with many people I know here in Miami. There is a boy in my son's class that cries when he gets anything lower than a 95! I feel like all this pressure it just setting kids up to fail. Or setting them up for a school life full of stress.

Summer of 2018

School has been out since the end of May which definitely alleviates the having to wake up to get to school stress. The difficulty now is getting her to wake up before 2:00 and get her to help do things around the house. Normal teenage struggles. She has always been a night owl and most nights she doesn't go to bed until anywhere from 12:00-2:00 in the morning. I have set a rule that she needs to wake up around noon and I do manage to get her out of bed by then on weekdays.

Her new medications have really made a difference as far as the depression goes. Her phobia is still there, but at least she is not suffering from the debilitating depression anymore. I think the phobia is going to remain with her for a long time. Dr. A was trying to do some gentle exposure therapy and work with her on spitting out soup into a bowl and then eventually in the sink and then into the toilet in her office building. It was really starting to throw my daughter over the edge and back into a depression, so we all agreed to stop that. It wasn't helping and it was just making her angry and more anxious. They are now focusing on coping skills and different ways to handle and manage her anxiety as well as life goals. We also keep up the rule that if she complains about her stomach hurting more than 6 times per day, she will lose her phone for the next day. That's down from the 20+ times a day she used to complain. It's a compulsion that is hard for her to control. Instead of the OCD actions she used to do, she has OCD thoughts and things she needs to say that are very hard for her to control.

Most of her coping skills were forgotten the other night when we saw a teenage girl run out of the restaurant where we had just had dinner and proceed to throw up on the sidewalk. We rushed to the car and my daughter was of course in a panic yelling for my husband to roll up his window and to hurry up and leave. I totally missed a good opportunity to not rush her away and to practice some coping skills, but it was such a whirlwind of anxiety that I couldn't even think straight since I knew she was going to freak out. It was a night for one of those back up pills called clonazepam that we have on hand for full blown panic attacks. It calmed her down and she fell asleep shortly after 11pm.

Hopefully we will be getting her medical marijuana card soon which may be a much better option for helping with the panic. We met with a doctor a few months ago and our application should be approved any day now. It's natural and it has properties that have been shown to greatly help stomach pains and anxiety. Once she starts, the doctor will be monitoring her closely to find the appropriate dosage of the cannabis oil. Our psychiatrist is very much on board and mentioned another patient she has with Crohn's disease. Medical marijuana has been the only thing that has helped his stomach and she is hopeful it will help my daughter as well.

This week we will be leaving for Austin, TX where my daughter will be training at Ballet Austin for three weeks at their summer intensive program. She will be going with her ballet friend from Miami and they will be sharing a room. She is excited yet nervous of course. Mostly nervous about someone getting sick. It will be easier than last summer since she will only have to share a bathroom with her roommate instead of a whole floor of other students. I am assuming I will be getting the dreaded multiple phone calls each day because she feels sick or has a headache or her friend is sick or has a headache. The good thing is that she will be in TX and I will be in FL and I don't have to answer my phone. It's so tiring having a child like this. I know there are so many parents who have it much worse than me, but never the less, it is exhausting and I can't wait to have a break!

Once she gets back home, school starts after a few weeks and then the whole college stress is going to start. We will continue to see Dr. A most likely through the remainder of high school. They have developed a relationship and I am sure my daughter shares much more with her than I know. I think it is good for her to have someone to talk to who has the skills and knowledge to teach and remind her of how to use her coping skills and other strategies. I feel like she is like a third parent that also helps me with strategies when problems arise. She has also been helping me to get her to investigate dance colleges that are not far away. My daughter desperately wants to be a dancer and I have explained that she has to go to college. She is not a strong enough dancer to get into any company straight out of high school.

My hope is that she gets into a college in FL that has a good dance program and she begins to explore other forms of dance besides ballet and maybe even some other interests as well. She needs to get out of her bubble in our home and experience life. Breaking that bubble is going to be tough but is must be done.

I hope you have found our story helpful. My one and only goal has always been to reach out to others who are in a similar situation. Struggling alone is awful and I remember it so clearly like it was yesterday. I believe that finding someone with the same struggle who can share their experiences and share what has helped and what they could have done differently is therapeutic in itself. You are never alone. It may not always be easy to find help or find someone who truly understands, but there are others out there.

About the Author

When a Child's Anxiety Takes Over is the first book Micheline Cacciatore has written. She grew up in Andover, MA and left for Salt Lake City in 1991 to pursue her pre-professional ballet training. When an injury ended her ballet career, she moved back to MA to attend photography school in Boston where she earned an associate degree in photography and met her future husband. After a few years as a professional photographer, she realized that ballet was her true passion and she began teaching and opened her own ballet school.

Micheline sold her ballet school in Massachusetts in 2010 so she could spend more time with her family and move to sunny FL. She still teaches ballet and lives in Miami with her husband, two children and three rescue dogs.

Made in the USA
Monee, IL
29 January 2025

11251444R00081